Before everything and everyone else, this book is dedicated to my mum.

This book wouldn't have happened without the most important woman in my life – the 5ft 10in, ginger, clumsy, level-headed backbone of our family. Yeah, quite a few of the recipes in this book have been passed down through Dad's side of the family, but they've all come to me from my white mum from Tottenham. Mum knows everything about me. She changed my life before anyone else did. My childhood is full of little memories of her doing things for us to make us happy, like walking into the kitchen on a Saturday evening where she'd be enjoying a glass of red while blasting George Michael and pulling pizzas out of the oven ready to sit together and watch Blind Date. Or tumble-drying my pyjamas on a Sunday night so, when I got out of the shower, I'd have warm crisp pjs to sit and watch Dream Team in. Sarah, thank you. Thank you, for cooking with me until 2 a.m., thank you for walking the dog when I didn't have time, thank you for believing in me when no one else did, thank you for never complaining about me battering the kitchen on shoot days. But mostly, thanks for being you babes. Everyone bloody loves you.

BIG HAS HOME

RECIPES FROM
NORTH LONDON
TO NORTH CYPRUS

HASAN SEMAY

PHOTOGRAPHY BY HARAALA HAMILTON

PAVILION

Welcome Home

When writing this book, I wanted the whole thing to feel personal, not just for me, but also for you guys as the readers. I don't feel like there are many personal touches in cookbooks nowadays. Yeah, we could have done this in a beautiful studio kitchen with props and backdrops, but like King Skeppy said, 'That's not me'. I wanted to keep the whole thing super raw because food is about togetherness, family, security, comfort and most of all HOME (see what I did there?).

Now, from the outside looking in, you're like, 'Has has made it, my man's got a book and shit'. However, that doesn't change a person's perspective. I'm not all of a sudden gonna wear a lumberjack shirt and change the way I carry myself. You're holding a book that I never thought would exist – I'm just as amazed as you are. Shit, I hope you're amazed, but thank you. I think being from the ends, we all have an underdog mentality. I was told I'd end up dead or in prison and I wasn't even that bad. I gave up on education and I guess education gave up on me. There was always a part of me that knew that I'd make it happen, cause I always do. So I guess this bit is an introduction to the ins and outs of my life/career, from the stationery-lacking, untucked-school-shirt, no-GCSEs bad boy to being an apprentice with Jamie Oliver at Fifteen (the asbestos hands grill-section guy and pasta-shape specialist), and now a published author.

I guess it all begins on 4 May 1991, when my poor mum gave birth to a whopping 5.5kg/10lb baby – to put that into perspective, my mum was carrying around eighteen packets of butter. I was born in north London, to a Turkish Cypriot dad and, after that birth, a somewhat battered English mum. I'm the youngest of three and was the most loved until my selfish sister decided to have kids of her own. Now, here comes that stereotypical line you always hear – 'Food's played a major role in my life', but if I'm being honest, it didn't really until I became a chef. I do have some great food memories – my grandma making me vegetable crisps when we had nothing else; my mum's coronation chicken and rice salad on almost every one of my birthdays; my cousin making bulgur kofte on our balcony in Cyprus; my Cypriot nan cutting everything with just her hands and a tiny little knife; watching my grandad milking goats on the farm; my dad taking me for adana kofte at Umut Ocakbasi on West Green Road and it being one of the best kebabs I've ever eaten; my brother-in-law introducing us to salt beef bagels with dangerous amounts of mustard.

I guess, for me, food is all about the 'feels' and capturing a moment in time – smells, flavour, the environment, the people around you and where you are on that day emotionally. Food is enchanting and captivating. Food swoons me. The best way to learn about culture is through food. I'm a sponge for culture; if I'm eating your food, I wanna learn your lingo, I wanna embrace your music, I wanna see the world from your perspective. Living in Edmonton, the Caribbean cultural influences ran deep, whether that was the yard shops on Tottenham High Road with their smoking drums out back, the older dons drinking Red Stripe outside Harry's cornershop or the guys driving around and banging out the slow, deep baseline of early ragga. *Play 'Under Mi Sensi'*

Like me, my close friend Robert was a sponge for culture; catching skin fades, listening to reggae and smoking the highest grade. You could play 10% of a reggae tune to Rob and he'd know it. Rob's one of my oldest friends, like real OG, batty and bench ting. Robert was always intrigued by Turkish culture from early on. He would eat his English mum's dinner and then come to mine for Turkish. He would learn Turkish songs word for

word, would always back a 'quick ting' lahmacun and now has a half-Turkish son. One summer, me and Rob spent almost every day together, sat in the garden, burning spliffs, talking life and lighting BBQs. Rob doesn't know how much he's helped me. Just listening when I needed him to listen, or telling me things that I already knew. In the early years of my career, Robert was my guinea pig. When I was about four years into my career and jobs were getting stressful, I could go check Rob, bun a spliff and persuade him to drive me to the fishmonger's in Enfield. I'll never forget the day I first introduced him to scallops. It was one of my rare days off and I'd hop on a bus up to Rob's, take off my shoes, greet the dog and then the family (because the dog would literally attack me with excitement), and walk straight to the fridge. When your peoples are your peoples, you are allowed to walk in and check the fridge. It's the first thing my friend Tayfun does when he comes to mine – that's family.

After scoping out the contents of Rob's fridge and not feeling inspired to make something, I roll a cheeky little zoot and we step out into his back garden. We leave the back door open so the reggae travels out with us. I take a couple draws on my spliff, eyes closed, face pointed to the sky, and think about what I would like to eat, to make my day great. 'Oi, Rob, you ever eaten a scallop?' Rob would often say things like, 'Nah, man, but I've seen them on Masterchef. Any good?' 'You know what would make today even better bro? A little fish BBQ and a beautifully seared scallop. What you saying?'

I never really go to the fishmonger with a plan – I like the idea of walking in and seeing what's fresh. On this particular day, it's a beautiful line-caught bass, stiff from rigor mortis with bright pink gills and super shiny eyes. When there's something super fresh and appealing, I don't care if it's my last tenner, it will always go on good food.

I leave the mongers with the star of my show and walk down the High Road to the market. It's a beautiful late-spring morning. I'm thinking fresh peas, asparagus, broad beans, mint, butter, lemon

zest and juice and parsley. EASY. I learned early on that the simplest dishes are always the hardest. If I overcook my asparagus and it's brown and floppy, or my fish is overcooked and dry, it's not going to work. I learned this from working in some pretty decent Italian restaurants. There's no fucking about – you source great-quality ingredients and cook them with precision 40–50 times a night. I'd say all of my food is like that now. I don't make it complicated.

Anyway, back to spliffs and sunshine. We get home and I set up the table outside, hit the spliff and play 'The vibes is right' by Barrington Levy. The vibe couldn't be any better and I'm in my element: tunes, check; sunshine, check; loved ones, check; BBQ, check. I sit in the sun with my

full attention on the bag of veg, taking broad beans out of their little designer jackets, peeling asparagus like I work in Bibendum. I make Rob pod the peas. He can't fuck that up. I blanch all my veg separately in heavily seasoned water. Changing the water each time. For me, blanched vegetables are how you should eat veg. Vegetables go into water at a rolling boil and, what I've learned over the years is, when the vegetable is at its brightest, it's done. When your peas go from that dull green to gorgeous tiny balls as green as grass, pull them out and stick them into iced water and let them cool off.

I move my attention to the BBQ Rob's already lit, and to this fucking day Rob lights BBQs the way my dad taught me. The now red-hot coals are

ready to make crispy bits of fish skin. I pat the fish dry, drizzle over veg oil and, with a huge crack of sea salt, rub it all over, from the tip of the head all the way down to the tail. Then I give my grill bars a little rub with lemon before putting the bass on to cook. An old shitty frying pan goes directly into the coals with a little splash of oil. I season the scallops generously until my pan's smoking. The scallops go in with a bit of pressure so the entire surface has contact with the pan, I flip after 1½ minutes to see that beautiful caramel colour on the underside. Pull the pan out of the fire and let the scallops chill on the side. New pan into the fire, huge knob of butter, let the butter foam, then in with all of my green bits, give them a roll around in the butter, season with salt and pepper, a little splash of water to loosen the butter and create a sauce. Flip my fish; it's got a leopard pattern from the direct heat between the smoking hot bars. I agitate my greens to get the butter to thicken. Add a huge squash of lemon off the heat so the acidity doesn't cook out, add some finely chopped mint and parsley. Green on to the plate first, beautifully grilled fish on top, a beautifully cooked scallop on the side, a little drizzle of olive oil. I look at Rob, he smiles, 'Go get knives and forks bro and turn the music down.' We sit, we eat, we vibe. Life's good.

For me, being a Turkish Cypriot and growing up with dual nationality plays a huge part in who I am. On the outside I look like a Turkish kid, but I grew up as a Londoner first. Saying that, I'd say we grew up in a pretty Turkish house, eating Cypriot food for dinner. My dad, Kamil, wasn't really open to change. He was born in Cyprus in the late 50s and was one of nine. He wasn't given a proper education and will tell you that he was a shepherd from the age of eight, walking hours away from his home with his goats.

He grew up with that village mentality – you work hard for something; you live off the land and protect what's yours. Dad was drafted into the Cypriot civil war at the age of seventeen. At the time, my family were living in what's now Paphos, on the Greek side. I'm not here to get all political and talk about the ins and outs of the war, because quite frankly I can't make sense of it. Greeks wanted Cyprus, Turks wanted Cyprus. It turned into a race thing; burning churches and mosques, the big cats got involved and people died. Sounds like most wars, right? The people making the power plays are all good and the bottom of the food chain have to deal with death, destruction and poverty. My dad was captured by the Greek army and was held as a prisoner for 96 days. Dad often tells me he was three days away from execution when the Red Cross burst through the door on some gang shit and saved them. I've never actually thought about what my dad's been through – he talks about it sometimes and I brush it off. But that guy had seen shit at eighteen that a lot of us won't ever see in our lifetimes.

My dad isn't really one for emotions. Until a few years ago, I was convinced that he'd had his tear ducts removed at birth. After the war, he lost all faith in his religion and his motherland and decided to leave Cyprus for London with his friend Hasan. He landed in the UK with £36 in his pocket and a packet of fags. He was met by his mate and taken to his cardboard-box of a room in dark and grey Black Boy Lane, Tottenham. Dad started off doing odd jobs – you know, the classic immigrant 'I'm a builder' speech. By this time, Tottenham already had established a decent little community of Greeks and Turks, so Dad felt somewhat at home. Dad meets Mum, the ginger goddess, in the Mayfair in Bruce Grove, not a city ting. Asks my mum for a dance and now I'm here writing this.

Saturdays were always the same for me growing up. Mum would be out with my sister, Alev, taking her to Dorothy Perkins and then off to see grandma. My brother, Arif, would be out at football or with his boys. I'd be left to my own devices, scrambling around the house to find some loose change to buy crisps and sweets from the shop. I'd spend the entire day watching cooking shows. The OGs; Ainsley, Gary, Keith, Rick and, obviously, Jamie Oliver. I wasn't ever really inspired to go off and cook after watching. In a way I was just really giving myself food blue

balls, growing more and more jealous of Rick Stein travelling around the south of Italy. I've wanted to be many things in my life. A DJ, a bed tester, a presenter, but when I fell for cooking shows, I wanted to be a TV chef. Although the food in these shows was always beautifully shot and heavily explained, I'd often skip through the dialogue just to watch the chef cook. Even then, I knew that food and food shows had an elitism around them. Cooking on Agas, beautiful backdrops, loud and expensive shirts. All that stuff wasn't aimed at kids like me, from lower-working-class backgrounds in the slums. I'd jokingly tell the boys that one day I was gonna be on the telly and make shows that we wanted to watch, with the same level of cooking but made more accessible. I've had the opportunity to do this but producers always want me to be that urban kid, to bridge the gap between them and my community, but it's always in a way that feels false, or as if someone has just googled the word

'urban' and chosen me. That's what birthed Sunday Sessions (big up George each and every time). Sunday Sessions is our baby.

Having left secondary school with a very small pot to piss in, the only chance of getting a job was teaching drama in France, so I enrolled at college to do a plumbing course to make my dad happy. But plumbing wasn't for me, and I soon found out that I couldn't fit in an airing cupboard, or under a sink for that matter. I then used my size to land a job as a security guard in an art gallery on the South Bank. I did this for two years and felt as if I was getting dumber. I handed in my notice and told the team I was going off to pursue my love of food.

Mum happened to be browsing the internet one day for catering courses when up popped an ad for Jamie Oliver's Fifteen – a training programme for young people deserving a chance. Me and mum sat for a good couple hours filling out an application form. I wasn't really paying attention to be fair, I never thought I'd get in. I remember getting an email back that was branded with the Jamie Oliver logo and was reluctant to open it. It was an invite to come in to Nile Street for a chat. My brother-in-law, Oli, took me in the back of his cab and I had a stomach full of emotions and anxiety. It didn't help that, when I got there, I was the only bellend wearing a suit. I instantly felt overdressed and uncomfortable but sat down for a chat and their opening line was, 'Nice suit, good to see you've made an effort.'

I left the interview not knowing how it went. It got to deadline on a sunny day in London. I'd spent the whole day in my garden smoking fags, answering texts from my mum with just the word 'no'. She'd never messaged me so much in one day. They said they would call between 9 a.m. and 5 p.m. No joke, at 5.15 p.m. my phone rings. Private number. 'Hi, is that Hasan? It's Tromie.' Hands sweaty, stomach playing drum and bass, fag already lit, pacing while on the phone. 'Good news, you're in.' Fam, honestly, I've not felt joy like that since. I remember looking up to the sky, sun on my face and giving it the tennis player fist shake and huge smile. This was it. The new beginning. The start of something I actually wanted to pursue, not because I had to or to make someone else happy. On the last day of our

first week we were told we had a special guest. In walks Jamie. When Jamie walks in, there's a presence, not like in a money way but the guy just radiates joy. I think I might have fancied him a touch. Who am I kidding? I still do. I remember him saying 'Here at Fifteen, we're family. We will always be here for you.'

The course was easily the best thing I have ever done. We spent three days of the week working in the restaurant alongside the chefs, doing the shit jobs like making stocks and chopping herbs, but I loved it. Then one day at college doing the boring paperwork side and learning how to make French sauces. We were taught things that chefs wouldn't see in a lifetime. Going down to suppliers, poultry farms, stroking cows, learning how to grow herbs. That's why I bang on about how important it is to support your local dealers. Chefs grow into that mindset, but at

Fifteen we were shown the ethos from the beginning, and I guess it's never left me. I'll drive to a proper butchers on the other side of London for a steak. Take the boys to the expensive fruit and veg shops where they watch me spend £70 in a matter of minutes. It was never done in a snobby way. For me, it felt like something we all should learn at school. However, it did make me a massive food snob. I remember coming home and saying to mum, 'Table salt is for boiling water, from now on we are seasoning everything with Maldon.'

For the first three months at Fifteen it was strictly Italian. Pasta, risotto, antipasti, baking bread and carpaccio. I enjoyed the rustic style and smell of an Italian kitchen. Chilli and garlic bleeding into olive oil to start the base of a fish dish, walking into the walk-in fridge to find huge wheels of Parmesan, the smell of the vines on a bunch of tomatoes or focaccia coming out the oven at 7.30 a.m. For me, Italian food almost felt like home. The difference between food in Cyprus and Italy isn't that great. Olive oil, aubergines, herbs, hard cheese, artichokes and the love of a humble tomato.

I owe a lot to Almir Santos, my Brazilian dad. Santos and Jamie had worked together at the River Café. Santos is tall, handsome, tanned, samba-obsessed, and with a Copacabana attitude. He is possibly the happiest guy I know – constantly smiling, taking the piss or shouting 'BUMMMMMBA' for no reason at all. I'd come in every morning and be the first apprentice on site and Santos would be in his office blasting samba or watching the highlights from the Brazilian league. I'd make us both a coffee and we would just chat until everyone else got in. I think the best time I spent with Santos was two weeks on the butchery section. It would be me and Santos in the back with the Kitchen Porters breaking down meat for the next couple of days.

Santos taught me everything I know about butchery. At the beginning, he would break the meats down into muscles and I'd trim off sinew. It gave us an opportunity to chat. Santos would often start conversations with, 'The ting is bruddah', with his hands held up like we were in the middle of surgery. 'You are born to be a chef my bruddah, just keep your head down and see the goal'. By the end of the two weeks on butchery, the roles had reversed. I'd be breaking down whole venison and Santos would be trimming. Me and Santos shared a moment when I graduated. He took me downstairs in the office and he just said, 'Your dad and my dad are the same guy – they love us no matter what. They may not tell you they're proud but trust me they're proud, my bruddah.' Those words have never left me. (Santi, I fucking love you, bro. Kiss to mum and Leo from me x)

I can't talk about Fifteen and not mention Jamie. When Jamie met my boys this year, all the mandem were like 'Jamie's just one of the mandem, innit', and he is. But he's more than that. Jamie Oliver is the reason you're reading this book; Jamie Oliver is the reason you know my name. Everything I've ever done; I owe to Jamie. He doesn't know how he's changed my life and every time I try to tell him, he's quick to change the subject. All those years ago, Jamie said that Fifteen is a family and last year I hosted my own supper club in his headquarters. It's all mad. Thank you bro.

After Fifteen, I spent most of my time in and out of Italian restaurants working with very talented chefs. Barnaby Benbow, my brother from another mother, who taught me for a stint at Fifteen and then got me a job at Rotorino in Dalston, became a member of my family very quick. Alex Jackson, who showed me how to cook a decent tomato sauce. Elliot Thomas, who figured out who I was and how I worked and took his time with me even when I was a moany prick. Massimo at Palatino, listening to me chat shit all day about ideas, food, sharing recipes. A big shout-out to Richard Blackwell for taking me on with my first sous role, showing the ropes, teaching me all the computer and clipboard side of being a manager. Also big shout-out to Stevie Parle, for just letting me be me, trusting me.

And I guess, after a eight-page long introduction to my life, that's pretty much it.

A Note on Ingredients

Listen, I know I bang on about sourcing quality ingredients but it's mad important. Ingredients that are looked after, grown or caught, just taste better. I don't get excited by loads of things, but a fish stiff with rigor mortis or fresh peas in the spring, really makes me happy. I know it's a little snobby and don't get it twisted, I still shop in supermarkets. I've not got a disposable income where I can blow racks in an independent greengrocer everyday, but for a couple of days a week you can catch me cooking something seasonal while my pocket weeps. Below is a list of some of the ingredients in the book you might not have heard of before and why you need to try them.

Olive oil - I use olive oil for seasoning, different types of olive oil have different characteristics. The bog-standard supermarket ones are like the people you meet on a night out and only talk to once; a good olive oil, however, with flavours of fresh-cut grass, rocket and artichoke will keep you entertained and wanting more.

Pul biber – is a dried chilli that's ground. It originates from Syria and is used commonly throughout Turkey and the Middle East.

Aci biber salçasi – is a spicy red pepper paste found in all Turkish supermarkets and households. It's not super hot but it's got a good hum. We use it mostly in stews, marinades or when cooking bulgur wheat.

Sea salt – I find seasoning with sea salt easier, it's flakes are bigger and you can see where they land. It's also a less intense, concentrated flavour than table salt.

Table salt – I only use table salt to season boiling water for pasta and blanching. Table salt is unforgiving.

Fresh beans – black-eyed beans, borlotti, coco de paimpol found in their little shells mid spring/early summer, these are all worth getting from the greengrocer.

Aci salgam – turnip juice traditionally drank after a kebab or along side raki. Personally, as a drink I find it a little intense, but it makes a good salad dressing. I reckon it would be quite nice on a hangover, it's got to be good for the gut or something.

Pastirma – Cypriot sausage, you can find it in most Turkish supermarkets with a butcher, but you can also use chorizo, which works just as well.

Chicken stock – there are a few recipes in the book that call for chicken stock. I like to make it up in a huge batch as you can then freeze it and use it when you need it. I like chicken stock to taste like chicken, no vegetables or herbs. I just take 4 chicken carcasses and 8 chicken wings and put them in a stock pot and add just enough water to cover. I then boil this for 10 minutes, until the water turns murky and scummy. I drain this off in the sink, saving the chicken in a colander and washing it under the tap. Then I return the chicken to a clean stock pot and cover with 6 litres/12½ pints water, which I bring to the boil and bubble away for an 1½ hours. When ready, I line a sieve with a cloth (it catches the smaller bits of chicken and most of the fat) and sieve the stock through it. Once cool, I stick it in the fridge or freezer. Simple.

Cheese – helim or as you might know it halloumi is pretty common now, it made it's way from strictly Cypriot shops into local mainstream supermarkets. It's also now being made by artisanal cheese mongers. Big up the mongers, kasar peyniri (cheese), beyaz peynir (white cheese), feta – they're all great.

Herbs – I know that the recipes in the book are precise weights, I don't cook like that normally but I want to make sure you guys finish up with the same end product as me.

Flowering oregano – grows commonly in Cyprus, it's floral and has more of a perfume. I like to use it to finish dishes but also whilst cooking. I get mine straight from the motherland out of my Hasan Amca's garden, but good Italian deli's always have it.

Amalfi lemons – grown along the Amalfi coast in Italy, they are full of juice and have a good balance between sweetness, acidity and that perfume-y flavour. It's definitely worth spending a little more cash on.

Sunsweet melon – they're super round, an off-grey colour, with a beautiful rubber band ball pattern exterior, you can smell them from miles away.

Tomatoes – bull's heart, tiger, datterini. It's always worth spending a little more money on tomatoes, there's a tomato for each season and every dish. I just love'em to be fair.

Cyprus potatoes – please try and find Cyprus potatoes, they're pretty common in the UK and sold in most neighbourhood veg shops. They're sweeter and less watery than other potatoes, so they are ideal for crispy chips.

Suzme or koy yougrt – strained yogurt - thicker and creamier than your everyday supermarket Greek yogurt, give it a try.

Pomegranate molasses – just pomegranate juice reduced down until it's thick and used as a salad dressing for a little tart sweetness, works great on sticky chicken wings, or to cut through a rich fatty piece of lamb.

Kirimizi toz biber – the Turkish version of paprika.

Tarhana – a dry powder made from a fermented mix of plain yogurt and wheat, used throughout Cyprus for what I'd say is our most common soup.

Fish – ask your fishmonger to gut and scale for you and to break the bloodline. If your local fishmonger smells, I wouldn't bother. It should smell of fresh sea water and the fish should be super shiny, a little stiff and have bright pink gills.

Eggs – always go organic, rich yolks have a deeper yellow yolk, they're fattier, give cakes and pasta doughs a better colour.

Dried porcini mushrooms – the caviar of the mushroom world. Easier to find dry but when they are fresh in the winter they're bloody great.

Kadayif – is just a really thick noodle made in Turkey and throughout the Middle East. Normally made from flour and water in a loose batter then piped onto a hot flat tray that cooks the thin strands super quickly.

Baldo Rice – is the most common rice eaten in Turkish households, its a member of the risotto family, wash off all the starch and cook it as you would a normal rice.

Pomace oil – is olive oil made from the remaining pulp of the more important presses. Basically, it's the last of the last, which is why it's cheaper and not so bitter.

Turkish ketchup – like most European ketchups comes in different variations, sweet, spicy and normal. It reminds me of holidays in Cyprus and I've always got a bottle in the fridge for nostalgia values.

TASTE IT BEFORE YOU PLATE IT

Is there enough salt? Is there enough acid? Is it looking a little dry? Writing recipes isn't a fool's guide to cooking. I don't want you just to follow the recipes and not understand how you've achieved them.

EQUIPMENT

Microplane grater - If you don't have one, I suggest you buy one, they're great.

A thermopen for BBQing - when starting to learn how to BBQ I feel like understanding the fire and heat is more important than anything else, however having a thermopen in your pocket is always a life saver.

A metal sieve for the BBQ - essential for blistering tomatoes over the fire.

A good non-stick pan for cooking fish. It will save your arse a million times.

Zig-zag pasta cutter - this is just to give your pasta that professional look.

Cook's blowtorch - I've always got a little blow torch by the BBQ just in case I need to top out the charcoal and get it lit quick.

Kebab skewers - invest in some proper stainless steel skewers most Middle Eastern grocery shops sell them in London. I like the square cut ones with the coiled ends.

BBQ - I'm not really into flashy BBQ's most of the recipes in the book were cooked on a BBQ that I've had for almost 11 years. BUT if you're gonna get yourself a BBQ, DRUMBECUES are fucking great and having a little portable joy stove goes a long way.

Pasta machine - I wouldn't bother splashing out on a full size one if you're just into cooking as a hobby but I'd recommend an "imperial" branded one.

How to Light a BBQ

OK, so throughout the book you'll hear me refer to 'counts' as this is how I was taught to measure the heat of a BBQ as a kid.

I'd sit with Kamil by the BBQ on a cold Sunday afternoon, both of us in fleece jackets, just watching him cook. In the beginning, I never really wanted to learn how to BBQ, it was more that, if I sat by the grill, I'd get all the good bits.

I have fond memories of watching Kamil, tea towel over his shoulder, marinating meat outside in the plastic box it came in, refusing to use fire lighters and only using a single fork to cook us all dinner. I don't often get on with Kamil, so while we're here, can I just explain why I call him Kamil?

Basically, as a kid I was a prick. I was always in trouble, whether it be at home or at school. Two particular days stand out for me when I think of Dad. The first one, I had a huge argument with him over some bullshit (common). We had had a go at each other – we're very similar as we both never back down. I've kinda grown outta that now – the older I've got, the more I've understood you've got to just let people be. Anyway, it kicked off, I went upstairs to play Pro Evolution Soccer on my ones. My dad burst through the door, 'Put your shoes on, get in the car'.

Reluctantly, I put my shoes on and Dad drove me 5 minutes up the road to a block in Edmonton called Isis (not the terrorist organization). At these sorts of times, Dad smoked fags like a chimney. He had been rolling this cigarette while driving, then pulled into a parking spot in front of the block of flats, let his window down and killed the engine. He took a big, deep sigh, lit his cigarette, turned to me and said, quite angrily: 'I'm FUCKING YOUR FATHER'. Possibly the best one-liner Kamil has come up

with. Not only is he my dad, but he's apparently also fucking my dad too. I couldn't help but laugh.

Obviously, it broke the ice and we made up. Dad said to me on the journey home, 'From now on, call me Kamil because I don't just want to be your dad any more, I want to be your friend. And that, ladies and gentlemen, is why I address my dad on a first-name basis – get out of my YouTube comments. Kamil's alright, I'm pretty sure he's still fucking my father.

Anyway, enough about the backwards incest *Star Wars* vision I've created. You guys are here to learn how to light a BBQ, how to maintain heat and be in control.

I still light fires the old-fashioned way, with fire lighters.

With the charcoal, build a little cone shape. Stack the pieces about 18cm (7in) from the base, putting pieces of charcoal on top of each other and using a mix of large and small pieces. It doesn't matter if there are gaps in-between the pieces, you need them for airflow to get the fire going.

Once you've got a rough cone shape, light a little piece of fire lighter and chuck it into the open hole at the top of your cone. Don't touch it, let it be. Allow your charcoal to get the red glow all the way through – no one wants seared sausage and food poisoning. Basic science: fuel + ignition + airflow = fire!

Cooking over live fire is more versatile than people think – you can cook low and slow or raging-hot, depending on where you stack your coals and what part of the grill you're using.

My old man taught me a basic rule. He stuck his hand out over the fire about 13cm (5in) from the grills and counted to 5.

If you put your hand over the fire and only get to a count of 1 before pulling your hand away in agony, that's a good temperature for charring veg.

A 2 count will cook fish super-fast and crispy (see page 107).

A 3–4 count is optimum temperature for red meat and thicker-cut steaks; still hot enough to get a good seal without fucking your presentation.

When cooking chicken, I always go for a 5 count, and especially if you're cooking boring chicken breasts.

I was always fascinated by my dad's hands; weathered and tough, and how he could turn pieces of meat with his bare hands. But I get it now – when you're a BBQ veteran, you don't need tongs. Kamil, *'Bana verdiğiniz ilham, coşku ve destek olmasaydı, bugün olduğum kişi asla olmazdım. Teşekkürler baba'.*

SMALL PLATES

Watermelon Salad

Watermelons are a big thing in Cyprus; eaten cold for breakfast out of the fridge, served room temperature with any lunch, or to mark the end of a meal. They are also used to bribe you into staying; there's no such thing as a flying visit with Turks or just popping in for a coffee. You'll kiss the same person goodbye at least three times and the entire family see the guests out. An auntie will shout, *'Gidemen simdi Halam, karpuz keseceyik'* ('You can't leave now, I've got watermelon to cut').

My dad taught me how to choose a good watermelon, what to look for and how they should sound. If you ever bump into Kamil standing over a pallet of watermelons, flicking each one twice, he's not gone mad, he's just trying to hear which ones are hollow. The hollow-sounding watermelons are at their ripest, under pressure, full of sweet fluid waiting to gush out. A good watermelon should almost crack when you first put a knife through it. I try to find the small Hey Arnold!-shaped watermelons; I often go for ones that have like a yellow 'birthmark' and sound like dropping something heavy into water when you hit them.

This is one of the dishes that introduced me to the similarities between Turkish and Italian food; Italians would use a salted ricotta for that salty, clean, acidic finish and us Cypriots use our bouncy, somewhat squeaky, helim.

SERVES 4

1kg/2lb 4oz watermelon
230g/8oz cherry tomatoes, halved
30g/1oz fresh red chillies
¼ bunch of coriander, leaves picked
¼ bunch of mint, leaves picked
zest and juice of 2 limes
3 tbsp good-quality olive oil (something deep and peppery)
50g/1¾oz helim or feta cheese (optional)
pul biber (see page 16, optional)
sea salt and black pepper

Cut the watermelon however you want – go for triangles, peel the whole thing like an orange and go for shards, or just scoop the flesh out with a spoon; whatever you can be bothered to do.

Slice the fresh chillies on an angle for a little flair, add to a bowl with the tomatoes and season generously. I like to season the tomatoes and chillies first to allow the tomato juice to run and the chillies to start to build their heat.

Go in with the watermelon next; toss it through the tomato and chilli juice with another little pinch of salt. Add the herbs, lime zest and juice and olive oil and toss again. Let the salad sit for a good 15 minutes; the longer the salad sits, the better it gets.

Plate up; I like to microplane some helim over the top, or crumble feta and scatter a generous pinch of pul biber for that little extra oomph.

Crab, Aioli and Summer Tomatoes

In the summer, I want light, citrus, delicate flavours and a glass of white wine. Fuck, I feel like Nigel Slater. I think it's because I'm a half warm-blooded Medi kid. Anyway, aioli is just a really punchy garlic mayo. Mayos aren't that easy to make; they're the one thing that I always struggled with and could only really make if I was running around like a headless chicken or really, really pissed off. So, let's take a breath, relax and take our time. You're not cooking for 150 customers with someone breathing down your neck. You're doing this for the love of good food. By all means go to your local fishmonger and buy picked crab for this recipe – not pre-dressed, as we're dressing it ourselves, and definitely not pasteurized – that stuff belongs in the bin.

SERVES 5

280g/10oz picked crab meat
280g/10oz summer tomatoes,
    such as small, sweet red and
    yellow Datterini and small Tiger
    tomatoes, halved
10 small basil leaves
peppery olive oil, for drizzling
sourdough, to serve (optional)

For the aioli
1 free-range egg yolk
130ml/4fl oz sunflower oil
80ml/2½fl oz good-quality
    extra-virgin olive oil
juice of 1 lemon
1½ garlic cloves
sea salt

First make the aioli. Place the egg yolk in a bowl and sit this on top of a tea towel; we're going to be whisking and don't want the bowl to move around. Pour the sunflower oil into a jug – you need one that will give you a slow, consistent pour. Start to whisk your egg yolk until it's completely smooth, then slowly pour in your oil for about 2 seconds at a time. We're trying to gradually build our emulsification (basically taking two fats that shouldn't mix – the egg yolk and oil – and manipulating them through whisking to hold together). DO NOT at any point get impatient and start adding loads of oil at once. You've been warned.

The egg yolk will start to stiffen and cling to your whisk, and you won't be able to whisk any more. At this point, you should have no oil left. Add the lemon juice and olive oil and whisk it in; your mayo will loosen up. I like a peppery olive oil in mayos as it gives you a kind of heaviness, which I feel a mayo needs. Grate in the garlic using a microplane (if you don't have one, I suggest you buy one – they're great) and season with a generous pinch of sea salt. Mix that in; I like my mayos tight, not loose, like the consistency of a 99 ice cream. If you like yours a little looser, add a tiny splash of water. When you taste your aioli it should be smooth, creamy and salty, with a BIG WHACK from the garlic, and finish with a clean acidity from the lemon juice.

Pick through the crab on a tray sat over ice – try to do this with some thin latex gloves on as there's an enzyme in our skin that starts to break crab down the more you touch it, plus we're trying to keep the crab as cold as possible. I do this in little sections; I'll split my crab meat into four bundles, then pat eight fingers down repeatedly in a line, feeling for any bits of skeleton or shell. I pick through each bundle of crab at least three times. I can guarantee you that each time you pick through it you'll find another piece of shell, so don't cut corners, it's soooo not worth it.

Place the tomatoes in a bowl, season super generously with salt and stir. Allow them to bleed their juices for about a minute, then add the basil leaves and give it a good splash of olive oil. Leave the tomatoes to rest with the handsome olive oil.

I just like to plonk bits of each component on the plate for this one. You should have more crab than anything else as that's the star. Eat as it is or build it like a bruschetta on really nice sourdough. If it's fresh, there's no need to toast. White wine optional, but heavily recommended.

Dressed Peppers

Roasted red peppers take a bog-standard BBQ to that next level. They're pretty easy to make, go well with meat and fish or are great just on top of a crusty bit of bread with loads of butter. By all means make this recipe with your classic red peppers, but if you can get your hands on those long red corno peppers use those. They're sweeter, cook better and the dark rich juice you get from steaming them after grilling is liquid GOLD.

SERVES 4

1.5kg/3lb 5oz sweet pointed
  peppers
100g/3½oz white onion,
  very thinly sliced
25g/1oz basil, leaves picked
80ml/2½fl oz good-quality olive
  oil
25ml/5 tsp sherry vinegar
10 anchovy fillets
sea salt
bread, to serve

Heat your BBQ so it's at a 1 count (see pages 18–19) and char your peppers. You don't want them completely blackened; if their skin goes jet black and starts to get that blue tinge, you've gone too far. You want the peppers to be soft on the inside. Constantly turn the peppers so that they don't develop too much colour. Once all the peppers are cooked and have turned limp and soft to the touch, pull them off the BBQ. Stick them in a bowl, cover with clingfilm and leave them to steam until they're completely cool.

Once cooled, peel the peppers. The easiest way to do this is to pull the stalks off, then turn the peppers so that you're holding them at the pointed end and slowly slide your hand down as if you're straightening your hair. Do it over a bowl so you can save all the smoky juices and keep the roasted peppers in as big pieces as possible, then set 'em aside in a bowl.

Add the sliced onions and basil to the peppers. Season generously with sea salt and strain the pepper juices over the top, then add the olive oil and sherry vinegar. Let the peppers sit for a couple of hours at room temperature – the vinegar will semi-pickle the whole mixture and take the harshness out of the onions.

Serve the peppers laid out on a plate, top with the anchovies and you're good to go. Get yourself some nice bread and mop up the juices.

Melon, Burrata and Prosciutto

OK, so maybe this one's a tad bit basic, BUT you can easily fuck it up. Shit melons taste like bin, supermarket prosciutto is for toasties and don't even get me started on brine-drowned burrata. In fact, maybe this should be the dish that you all try, to understand what food sourced right can be. I know that last sentence makes me sound super snobby, but when ingredients are at their peak, produced by people who care and seasoned correctly, the results are something else. Back in the day, I put this exact dish on as a special at Palatino and Richard Blackwell, my head chef at the time, told me I was crazy. It sold out in just under an hour.

This is a vibe on a late summer evening. You know, that point where you've finally regulated your body temperature, you're sat in the garden listening to easy tunes, having the time to take everything in, and secretly being eaten by mozzies. This dish was made for that time.

I cannot stress the importance of buying a Sunsweet melon from Mantua, Italy. I bought two while testing this recipe, obviously I knew I didn't actually need two, I was just happy to have one sat on the windowsill and have the kitchen smell like Grandma's house in Cyprus. There's two smells that always take me back to Cyprus and they're both centered around my nan's house. One is the smell of jasmine walking up the marble stairs to her front door and two is the smell of watermelons ripening in the sun in her kitchen.

SERVES 2 OR 1 HASAN

500g/1lb 2oz Sunsweet (see page 16)
    or Cantaloupe melon
10 slices of prosciutto
125g/4½oz burrata
pul biber (see page 16)
good-quality extra-virgin olive oil
sea salt

I like to ripen my melon in the sun for a good couple of hours; it just makes the melon feel at home. When it warms up, all the juice gets to run through the fibres again, giving us the best melon possible. Cut the melon open, take a second to enjoy the smells, then cut it how you normally would. And stick it on a plate.

I don't even bother trying to make prosciutto look pretty; just let it fall on itself naturally.

I like to eat this with fridge-cold burrata, topped with a crack of salt, pul biber and a good glug of oil. If I'm being totally honest, this isn't something I like sharing. I'll happily eat the whole melon and all the prosciutto and feel no way bad about it.

Squid and Smashed Tomatoes

I love grilled squid – the sweet smell as it hits the charcoal, the way it turns from translucent to opaque – it's even kind enough to let you know when it's cooked. No frozen squid here please, go to the fishmongers and get it fresh, and get them to clean it for you.

SERVES 3

750g/1lb 10oz squid
2 garlic cloves, grated
1 tsp fennel seeds
25ml/1fl oz olive oil, plus extra for drizzling
300g/10½oz Tiger tomatoes or Datterini
   cherry tomatoes
sea salt

For the dressing
2 anchovy fillets
15g/½oz mint, leaves picked and chopped
20g/¾oz flat-leaf parsley, leaves picked
   and chopped
 20g/¾oz basil, , leaves picked and
   chopped
juice of 2 limes
30g/1oz chopped pistachios, chopped
good-quality olive oil
sea salt

To serve (optional)
chopped chives
pul biber (see page 16)
lemon wedges

Prepping the squid is pretty simple – you should have a nice clean, white, cone-shaped piece of squid and tentacles. Trim the wider end off so it's nice and straight. If you look in the squid tube, you'll notice there's a little grove where its quill sits (the bit of plastic that allows the squid to stand up right). Roll the squid so the groove is facing away from you and, with one smooth motion, run your knife against it. The squid will fan out, and more than likely there will still be a few bits of gunk, so scrape these away with a butter knife and rinse under the tap. Do this to all the squid beforehand, otherwise you'll be there for ages doing them one by one. Cooking is about working smart and not hard. Once all your squid is fanned out and clean, pat it dry with a clean cloth (we don't want any moisture in our marinade). Score the squid with the same butter knife on a 45-degree angle, scoring in opposite directions to give you a diamond pattern. I like to make loads of little lines just so we can pick up as much dressing as possible.

Marinate the squid and tentacles in a bowl with the garlic, fennel seeds and olive oil. I only do this for about 1 hour in the fridge – it doesn't need long.

Light your BBQ following the instructions on pages 18–19.

You'll need a pestle and mortar for the dressing; food processors are great for most things, but I usually stay away from chopping herbs in them because they bruise the herbs and release moisture. Start off by adding the anchovy fillets to the pestle and mortar and breaking them down into a paste. Then add your chopped herbs and a good crack of salt. Smash the herbs down until they're a fine paste, add the lime juice to cut through the salt and make the colours of the herbs pop. Add the chopped pistachios and enough olive oil to cover. We want the dressing to be a spooning consistency – we don't want to drown it with oil, we just want the olive oil to bring everything together.

I like to blister tomatoes over fire using a sieve; you get a smoky sweetness and I also like the way cooked tomatoes retain their juices and lose their acidity. Cut the tomatoes in half, season with salt and a little glug of olive oil and put them in a big metal sieve. Find a nice little 3 count (see pages 18–19) somewhere and let the tomatoes slowly cook down.

Grilling squid has to be hard and fast. All the little scores in the squid are going to go a beautiful caramel colour and have that roasted shell flavour. I lay my grills directly on the coals for this. We are looking at a solid 1 count; no messing around.

The squid has been in the fridge so the olive oil will have solidified – give it a little extra glug of olive oil and mix it through. The fat from the oil is going to give us smoke and more flavour. Season each piece of squid and tentacle individually, don't just put the salt in the bowl and hope for the best. You can hope for the rest of your life, but you'll always have a few bits that have been neglected. Pay attention to where the salt is landing on your squid. You want a good even coating so that each bite is seasoned. Do the same with the tentacles – those are my favourite bit.

So now you've seasoned each bit of squid, your tomatoes are slowly cooking away and your grill has been sat on your raging-hot fire for about 5 minutes. Go on with the tentacles first. The tentacles need a little longer and I like to get a really good char on them so there's a little texture. Once you've put them on the grill, you are not to move them until the tentacles give you the all-clear. They'll retract under the intense heat and start to spread and curl.

People often ask me why I sit when I'm grilling: one, it's because I've spent eleven years standing up for 80 hours a week, and two it's because I'm closer to the action. Being 6ft 6in, everything is super low down – it's like sitting in row Z at Wembley. If I'm sat down I can focus on what's happening. The tentacles will start to caramelize; you'll smell the change in the air, from the sea to sweet, and you'll get little pockets of fragrance from the fennel seeds releasing their oils. At that point, and that point only, you can flip them. You should have beautiful crispy, opaque tentacles.

Once you've flipped the tentacles, add the rest of the squid to the grill. Again, wait for the smells. The scored squid is easier to judge as you'll notice it change colour straight away. The way I tell it's ready is the little diamond shapes that we have cut into the squid will start to puff up, the lines we have cut will stay flat, and the corners of your squid will start to fold. Now you're getting sweetness in the air, fennel seeds toasting again. Flip the squid and cook it on the other side until it's fully curled – it will only take about 15–20 seconds – then pull everything off the grill.

Chop the squid into little bite-sized rings and the tentacles in half. Add them to a fresh bowl (try using metal as the squid will retain its heat), then add your blistered tomatoes and your dressing. Mix it together. TASTE IT BEFORE YOU PLATE IT.

Eat a piece of dressed squid. You should get soft squid, saltiness from the seasoning and the anchovies in our dressing, sweetness from the tomatoes and caramelized squid and it should finish with vibrancy and acid. If you have all of that, you're good to go; if not, figure out what it is you're lacking and add more.

Plate it; I like a few chopped chives on the top of mine, another little drizzle of olive oil, a little scatter of pul biber and a wedge of lemon.

Sea Bass Carpaccio

Carpaccio is all about the quality of the fish; the first time I made it was at Rotorino in Dalston with the greats. It was on the first summer menu and most of the time it was cut to order because we were in the shit. It taught me the importance of seasoning correctly; how delicate food can be; how so few ingredients can make something stupidly delicious and how you can't do shit with a blunt knife in a kitchen.

You can't make this with a fish from a supermarket and I don't care if it's an expensive supermarket with a fish counter. Support your local fishmonger, ask them for something line-caught, that's not been force-fed or eaten chemicals. We want something stiff out of the ocean, eyes still beaming. FISH DOESN'T STINK, SHIT FISHMONGERS DO!

SERVES 2

105g/3¾oz line-caught sea bass
    (about 1 fillet)
30g/1oz orange
30ml/1fl oz lime juice
30ml/1fl oz lemon juice
a tiny pinch of sugar
4 red Datterini tomatoes
4 yellow Datterini tomatoes
good-quality olive oil, for drizzling
sea salt

I don't bother curing my fish – when your fish is spanking fresh, it doesn't need it and we want the fish to sing in all its glory. Make sure your knife is super sharp, otherwise you'll make a dog's dinner. I've never asked my monger to slice the fish for me, but if you ask nice enough, maybe they will. Slice the fish as thin as you can get it, while trying to keep it in whole slices – you want to be able to see through it if you hold it up to the light. When working with fish, it's about long strokes and using the whole length of your knife. Whether that's filleting, portioning or making cute little slices because some big handsome Turkish guy told you to. We want even cuts – it makes the end product look that much better. Lay the fish out on a plate, trying to keep all the slices flat, although a little overlapping won't hurt.

Top and tail the orange and cut away the rind, exposing the flesh all the way round. Cut out the segments, then cut each segment into four pieces and squeeze the juice out of the remaining orange in to a bowl for the dressing. Add the lemon juice and lime juice to the orange juice with a little pinch of sugar.

Season the fish on the plate with sea salt and spoon over enough dressing to cover, squash the tomatoes on to the plate, breaking the flesh and scattering around. If there are any younger leaves in your basil, use those; if not, tear a few of the bigger ones over the top. Scatter your orange segments about the plate so that, if someone picks up a piece of fish, they get a little of everything. Drizzle over some nice olive oil and let the fish sit for about 5 minutes. The longer the fish sits, the more cured it will be. If you want a harder bite to your fish, let it sit in the acid for about 15 minutes, but I like to enjoy it sooner rather than later.

Ezme

Another kebab-shop classic. I prefer a spicy ezme to bog-standard kebab-shop chilli sauce. I enjoy watching the chef get really pissed off when you order one on a busy night too. I know how you feel bro, I feel your pain. Also, when was the last time you sat down to eat in a kebab shop? The last time I went I was given a basket of bread and a little pot of garlic and chilli sauce – what the fuck's that about? I don't need this now. That's for later 'my fren'.

SERVES 6

2 sweet pointed peppers
2 small cucumbers
2 medium tomatoes, peeled
4 spring onions
6g/⅛oz sea salt
1 tsp sumac
½ tsp smoked sweet paprika
20g/¾ oz flat-leaf parsley
5g/⅛oz mint leaves
130ml/4fl oz good-quality olive oil
30ml/1fl oz good-quality balsamic
     balsamic
60ml/2¼fl oz pomegranate
     molasses
4 Bullet chillies, super finely
     chopped

Basically, finely chop all the peppers, cucumbers, tomatoes and spring onions individually, then run your knife over them until they are super fine. Add them all to a bowl. Add in the salt, sumac and smoked sweet paprika. Chop your herbs as fine as you can get them, then add them in next. Then add the olive oil, balsamic vinegar and pomegranate molasses.

The Bullet chillies make the ezme pretty spicy, so feel free to leave them out and use it more as a salsa than a chilli sauce, otherwise mix them through and enjoy.

Atom

Essentially, we are making labneh in this recipe, which is a strained yogurt that is served as a cold starter in restaurants around Turkey and the Middle East. I find this works best with a clean pair of tights, but if you happen to have something more appropriate knocking about – like cheesecloth or muslin – then go with that.

SERVES 2

650g/1lb 7oz thick yogurt (try and
   get Turkish stuff labelled
   'suzme')
5g/⅛oz sea salt
15g/½oz caster sugar
2 garlic cloves, grated
juice of 1 lemon

For the pul biber brown butter
60g/2¼oz good-quality unsalted
   butter
2 tbsp pul biber (see page 16)

Spoon out the yogurt into a bowl and add the salt, sugar, garlic and lemon juice. Give the yogurt a good mix and scrape it into your fabric of choice. I hang mine in the garden for at least 2 hours and allow gravity to work its magic. The longer the yogurt is left to hang, the stiffer it becomes – we want it to be a cream cheese consistency.

For the pul biber brown butter, melt the butter in a saucepan over a medium heat and, just as the kitchen starts to fill with butterscotch smells and you have a slight golden colour on your butter, go in with the pul biber. It's important to catch the butter just at the beginning of the brown butter process; if the butter is too hot, it will fry off the deep flavours from the pul biber. Once the pul biber is in, give it a little swirl and take it off the heat. We want the pul biber to infuse and bleed out its colour and flavour.

When the yogurt is ready to serve, I like to literally whack it on to a plate and create a little dip in the middle that our hot butter can sit in. Or you could keep the yogurt in the fridge for up to three days, but if you've added the butter on top, it's best served immediately.

Cold Kebab-Shop Aubergine

You know when you sit down in Turkish restaurants and you sometimes get that cold aubergine and potato thing to dip your bread in, well we call that *saksuka*. I know you lot think that's got baked eggs in, but this is the kebab-shop-style one. Also, mine's better. Big man ting.

SERVES 4

600g/1lb 5 oz aubergines, cut into 2.5cm/1in cubes
1.5 litres/2¾ pints vegetable oil
200g/7oz long green peppers, cut into 2.5cm/1in cubes
300g/10½oz potatoes, peeled and cut into 5cm/2in cubes
3 garlic cloves, sliced
60ml/2¼fl oz olive oil
500g/1lb 2oz good-quality fresh tomatoes, such as beef or oxheart, grated
2 tsp aci biber salçasi (see page 16)
1 tsp pul biber (see page 16)
1 tsp caster sugar
sea salt

Heavily salt your aubergines and let them sit in the salt for at least 20 minutes to draw out the moisture.

Heat the vegetable oil in a heavy-based cast-iron pan or saucepan (you can also do this in a deep fryer, just make sure the oil is clean). You want the oil to be about 180°C/350°F. Pat the aubergines dry before frying to prevent them spitting back at you. Fry the aubergines for 8–10 minutes until brown on all sides, then allow them to drain on a rack or on top of some kitchen paper. Although we used salt to draw out the moisture, we need to season them again while they're still hot.

Fry the peppers in the same pan for 5–7 minutes until they're soft and the skin is blistered, then allow them to drain and season while they're hot.

Place the potato cubes in heavily salted water and boil until they're just done. If you overcook them, when it comes to mixing everything together, the potatoes will break down and make the mixture thick and floury. Set all of this stuff aside and leave it cool.

Basically, all we gotta do now is make a tomato sauce, mix everything together and we're done. Fry the garlic gently in the olive oil in a wide frying pan – a wide frying pan just means it will cook quickly. (Surface area + heat = shit cooks quicker; I learned that being in the shit in service and often trying to reduce a sauce to order.) You want the garlic to fry gently with no colour – give it a couple minutes and add the aci biber salçasi and pul biber, then let that fry off for a couple of minutes – we just want to bring it up to temperature and cook the rawness out of it. Add the grated tomatoes and turn up the heat to bring them to the boil. Cook your sauce for about 15 minutes, cooking out the raw liquid until you're left with a smooth sauce. Add the sugar and season with salt.

Remove from the heat and allow to cool before mixing all the vegetables and sauce together, trying not to break up the potatoes. Let it sit in the fridge overnight – the longer it sits in the fridge, the better it gets; however you have three days maximum to eat it.

Purslane, Walnut and Feta Salad

When we were kids, in early summer, my dad used to make a salad of purslane, beef tomatoes, red wine vinegar and dried mint. It was the best thing to dip the bread in after a kebab. This idea is born off the back of that. Also, it's not sea purslane, just purslane. You can get it in spring and early summer in most Turkish shops. Just look for *semiz otu*.

SERVES 2

1 bunch purslane, washed (80g/2¾oz)
1 Cuore del Vesuvio tomato or a handful of really nice cherry tomatoes
4 sprigs of mint
40g/1¼oz walnuts
60g/2¼oz feta cheese
good-quality olive oil, for drizzling
30ml/1fl oz pomegranate molasses
juice of ½ lemon
sea salt

Pick the purslane off the stalks and into a bowl – try to pick the leaves so they are still together in their little bunches, it eats better with that little bit of stalk holding it together. Cut your tomato in half and then chop each half four times. I don't do this uniformly – I like some longer bits than others.

Add the tomatoes to the purslane in the bowl. Pick the mint leaves in and just leave them whole. Crush the walnuts in your hands and add to the bowl. Do the same with the feta. Season with a good crack of salt. Drizzle over enough olive oil to dress the leaves but not drown them. Add the pomegranate molasses and lemon juice. Toss all the ingredients together and serve.

Charred Beetroot

This is one that I learned while working at a Turkish restaurant in Baker Street and I've made it a few times since and changed it a tad here and there. It's a really pretty dish and it makes complete sense. Earthiness from the beetroot, depth from the confit garlic, vibrancy from the mint, sweetness from the pomegranate molasses and sourness from the fresh feta. Just a good one to rock up to a BBQ with and show people how versatile veg is.

SERVES 4

200g/7oz golden beetroot (you
   can use whichever type you can
   get but I like the earthiness of
   the golden ones)
1 tbsp confit garlic oil
4 tsp pomegranate molasses
50g/1¾oz feta cheese
6 mint leaves
20g/¾oz toasted hazelnuts,
   roughly crushed
sea salt

For the confit garlic oil
180ml/6fl oz vegetable oil
1 garlic bulb, peeled

To make the confit garlic oil, place the oil in a saucepan, add the garlic bulb and cook over the lowest heat until it comes to the boil. Then poach it slowly in the oil – we don't want the garlic to take on any harsh colour, we want to cook it super gently for 45 minutes–1 hour. Once finished, stick it in a jar and it will last for months as long as the garlic is under oil.

Get your BBQ ready (see pages 18–19). There isn't really a count for this one, so once your coals are hot, stick your beetroot in the charcoal. The heat is intense so you need to keep your eye on them and turn them as they start to char on the outside and look like ash. Cook the beets all the way round, including the tops and bottoms.

Like when cooking peppers, we need to let our beetroot steam and rest as they will continue to cook out of the coal. I know you're thinking, 'How do I know when they're cooked?' Well, slip a skewer through them and there should be ever-so-little resistance – we don't want to cook them to shit, we still want a bit of an al dente feel when we eat them. Remove from the heat and leave the beets until they're cool enough to handle.

Using a damp cloth, peel away the burnt outer crust until you can see the beetroot underneath. Slice the beetroot as thinly as you can – I do mine on a mandoline but be careful of your fingers as they are bloody lethal. Once sliced, lay the beetroot on your serving plate – you want the slices flat but it doesn't matter if they're overlapping.

The rest is just dressing the plate. Crack over salt so that a bit is sat on top of almost every slice. Drizzle over the confit garlic oil and pomegranate molasses and crumble the feta over the top. Stack the mint leaves on top of each other, roll the stack up and slice through it as thinly as you can. Scatter this over the top and finish with the roughly crushed hazelnuts.

Helim, Sausages, Pickled Shallots and Honey

These are two things that we grew up on as kids. Mum wouldn't let us eat pastirma often as she said, 'It makes the house smell like garlic and lamb'. Mum's not a huge fan of lamb and also never used garlic until I became a chef as she claimed it made her smell. That's changed now – Mum always smells like clean linen and eats garlic in almost everything I make.

SERVES 3

2 pastirma (see page 16) or
    chorizo sausages
250g/9oz block of helim
olive oil
1 tbsp honey
juice of ½ lemon
dried flowering oregano
a small bunch of chives,
    finely sliced
sea salt

For the pickle
350ml/12fl oz red wine vinegar
5 tbsp caster sugar
1 tbsp sea salt, plus extra for
    seasoning
4 banana shallots, cut in half
    lengthways (skin on)

Start off with the pickle. Put all the ingredients except the shallots into a saucepan with 175ml/6fl oz water, bring to the boil, then turn off the heat and set aside.

Heat a dry frying pan until it's just starting to smoke, then rub a little oil and sprinkle some salt on the fleshy side of your shallots. Stick your shallots in the pan, exposed-side down, and don't move them. We want the shallots to colour as this is going to give our pickle extra dimension and make it a little less harsh. Char the shallots for about 4 minutes until they are completely blackened, then turn them over and turn off the heat. Let the residual heat in the pan cook the other side of the shallots. I add my pickle liquor to the pan while the pickle is still hot so the shallots can sit in it while it's warm and take the edge off. Let the shallots sit in the pickle for at least 3 hours. Just remember to take the skins off them before you serve.

Peel the skins off the pastirma – the easiest way to do this is to make a slit along them lengthways and peel the skin off under cold running water. The water makes the skin tighten and easier to peel. Cut each sausage into four equal rounds.

Take the helim out of the packet, give it a rinse under the tap and cut it into four equal slices, about finger-width.

Stick a little glug of olive oil into a frying pan over a medium heat and add your pastirma. Treat the pastirma like chorizo, let the oil bleed out but don't worry about cooking it all the way through as it's cured. I let mine slowly fry for about 5 minutes, getting it a little bit crispy. Stick your pastirma in a bowl and set aside.

Give the same frying pan a little wipe and add another glug of olive oil to cook the helim. Fry over a medium heat for about 3 minutes on each side, until it's golden and crispy.

Add the pastirma back to the pan with the helim, along with the honey. Squeeze in the lemon juice and scatter over some flowering oregano. Let the honey bubble for about 30 seconds. Stick the helim and pastirma into a serving bowl along with their cooking juices. Add a few petals from the pickled shallots. Finish with a scattering of chives over the top. Eat with a nice bit of bread or enjoy on its own.

Roasted Tomatoes and Labneh

Leftover labneh from the other recipes; I got your back. I made this originally as a snack and thought it was book-worthy. Confit tomatoes last a good while and, if you don't have labneh, they're just great on bread anyway.

SERVES 4

400g/14oz mixed cherry
    tomatoes on the vine
1 peeled garlic bulb
100ml/3⅓fl oz good olive oil
a bunch of basil, plus extra
    for serving
leftover labneh
bread of choice; I went with
    a doughy flatbread
2 tbsp black sesame seeds,
    for scattering
sea salt

Preheat the oven to 160°C fan/180°C/355°F/gas mark 4.

Take your cherry tomatoes off the vine and place them in a shallow tray with the garlic and olive oil. Roast in the oven for 35–45 minutes, until the skins just start to blister.

Turn the oven off and add in the entire bunch of basil, stalks and all. I let the tray sit in the warm oven for a couple of hours. Once cooled, you can then transfer the tomatoes to a jam jar and, as long they're under oil, they'll keep in the fridge for at least a month.

The rest is an assembly job really. Smear a good spoonful of leftover labneh across a nice piece of warm bread. Add your tomatoes over the top and give them a squish, plus I like to drizzle over a little bit of the oil the tomato has cooked in. Hit it with some fresh basil for vibrancy, a pinch of salt and a little scattering of black sesame to bring a little contrast.

Breakfast, lunch or a cheats dinner. It goes a long way.

Fried Courgette Flowers

This is just one of those cute little starters and great with cold cocktails on a summer's day. Yeah, it's a bit bouji finding courgette flowers, stuffing them and frying them but, honestly, they're so different and delicious everyone will love them.

SERVES 4

10 courgette flowers
sunflower oil, for frying
sea salt and black pepper
lemon wedges, to serve

For the batter
550ml/20fl oz cold sparkling water
250g/9oz plain flour

For the filling
2 anchovy fillets
240g/8½oz ricotta
2 thyme stalks, leaves picked
zest of 1 lemon
15g/½oz Parmesan cheese, grated
a crack of sea salt and black pepper

If you're lucky enough to be growing your own courgettes, cucumbers, melons or squash flowers, then great. If not, you can find them in high-end greengrocers in the late spring and early summer. Also, don't be scared to ask your grocer to order things in for you – pretty often they're up for it.

For the batter, make sure your sparkling water is super cold – you can make the batter in advance and leave it in the fridge for 30 minutes or so. Just give it another mix before using. Add your flour to a bowl, then slowly add your sparkling water, whisking until the batter resembles single cream. Dip one of your fingers into the batter and it should just coat your fingertip lightly.

Start off by removing the little pollen stem in the middle of the courgette flower. The flowers are super delicate. I find the easiest way to get them to open up is just to give them a little blow and get your finger inside it while it's open. It doesn't matter if you split the walls of the flower too much – our batter is going to act as a barrier to the inside of the flower.

To make the filling, break the anchovies down in a pestle and mortar, then transfer to a bowl, add the remaining filling ingredients and give them a good mix. Stick your filling in a piping bag.

Blow into a courgette flower again, then get the end of the piping bag into the flower and fill just the green parts. Don't fill them all the way to the top as the orange tips will stick together when they're dipped in the batter and act like a safety blanket.

Fill a deep-fryer with clean oil and preheat to 170°C/338°F. Once the oil is hot enough, dip the flowers into the batter one by one, then gently drop them into the oil. Fry on one side for about 2 minutes – the flowers will slowly start to turn once the underside is crisp. Give them a little turn and fry for another 2 minutes. Once crisp, transfer the flowers to a plate lined with kitchen paper to catch any excess oil. Season.

Plonk them on a plate with a nice wedge of lemon and eat them while they're still hot and crispy.

CYPRIOT DISHES

Lamb
and
Potato
Kofte

My mum hates deep-frying at home – 'makes my hair stink' or 'all my clean washing smells like a chip shop' – so this isn't a dish we get to eat very often at mine, but that's probably why I like it so much. As we touch down in Cyprus, the aunties battle it out to be the first to have us over and they all know that this is a heavy hitter for me. Traditionally, these little lamb and potato koftes are served with freshly boiled black-eyed beans and mountains of yogurt.

Please try and find Cyprus potatoes – they're pretty common in the UK now and are ideal for crispy chips.

SERVES 4

For the kofte
1.4kg/2lb 13oz potatoes (ideally
    Cyprus, see page 16)
35g/1¼oz sea salt
12g/½oz freshly ground black
    pepper
2 tsp cumin seeds, crushed
1 tbsp pul biber (see page 16)
2 large onions, grated
700g/1lb 9 oz minced lamb
    shoulder
sunflower oil, for frying
a bunch of flat-leaf parsley, finely
    chopped

For the black-eyed beans and spinach
500g/1lb 2oz black-eyed beans
    (see page 16)
260g/9 ½oz spinach, chopped
300g/10½oz shallots, finely diced
juice of 2 lemons
sea salt
good-quality extra-virgin olive oil

Pod the black-eyed beans as you would peas or broad beans, leaving any smaller ones in the pods as we can just cook these as is. Add the beans to a saucepan of water and boil for 5 minutes – we just wanna get all the gunk off them and slowly start to soften the outer skins.

Drain off the murky water, give the beans a little rinse, put them back in the same pan, with cold water, and bring to the boil. Now, depending on how fresh your beans are, you need to slowly simmer them from anywhere between 25 and 45 minutes. We want the skins to be soft and to taste a smoothness in the beans' interior when biting down on them.

While the beans are cooking, make the kofte: Grate the potatoes on the fine side of a box grater; I like to do it on their longest side. Once all your potatoes are grated, drain off all the moisture using a tea towel or some muslin.

Add the potatoes to a large bowl, season with the salt, black pepper, cumin and pul biber. Add the grated onions with their juice and then the minced lamb and parsley and give it a good mix. I like to mix it for at least 5 minutes; don't just use your hand as if it was a spoon – squeeze the mix through your fingers and make sure everything is evening distributed. In Cyprus we just shape these into little torpedoes or small meatballs. It's up to you.

When the beans are cooked, add your spinach and take the pan off the heat. Spinach is soft and will pretty much wilt in the sun, so it doesn't need long. Don't leave the spinach in the water for too long or you'll just drown it and lose all the flavour in the water. Drain the beans and spinach and set aside.

In a little frying pan, sweat down your finely diced shallots really slowly in olive oil and with a good amount of salt. Sweat them down for about 15 minutes until they're soft and sweet without any colour.

In a tall-sided frying pan or saucepan, heat enough oil to cover half the kofte. We don't want to deep-fry them but shallow-fry and turn them midway through cooking. If you deep-fry the kofte, the heat is too intense, and the potatoes won't cook. Be patient, they'll take about 4–5 minutes on each side or until

they're a beautiful golden brown. You'll never want a plain old hash brown ever again.

By now, the shallots should be sweet and the beans and spinach shouldn't be steaming hot, so put everything in a bowl. (If your beans are still super hot, you've not cooked your shallots long enough.) At this point, you need to taste the mixture and you'll probably find it's a little flat – you'll have a little saltiness but nothing will really be singing. Squeeze in the lemon juice and taste again. Now the acidity is up, our tongues are entertained and you want to mellow that acidity out with peppery olive oil.

Add olive oil not as if you were dressing a salad, but more like you're using the oil as a flavourful ingredient. A lot of Cypriot dishes are oil-heavy. It's all about balance; olive oil in Cyprus is made from black olives so it can be quite heavy, but when you're cooking something as basic as beans, spinach and shallots, you need something that's gonna carry flavour and give you that power. You want to be able to see the olive oil on the plate – that's the good stuff that bread was made for.

Plate up the kofte and beans and spinach with some yogurt and bread. Welcome to Cyprus.

Bezelye

SERVES 5

1kg/2lb 4oz diced lamb leg (ask the butcher to take it off the bone and keep the bone)
olive oil
2 large white onions, diced
300g/10½oz carrots, sliced into rounds
500g/1lb 2oz fresh peas
2–3 tbsp tomato purée
2 x 400g/14oz cans whole tomatoes, drained
sea salt and black pepper

To serve
rice
Turkish yogurt
nice bread

First season your diced lamb. Next, place the oil in a deep, flameproof casserole dish and bring it up to temperature over a medium heat. Add the diced lamb in batches; the trick is don't overcrowd your pan when browning meat. It's all about keeping heat in the pan, building that dark crust and starting to flavour the oil with lamb fat. Also, we don't want to burn any of the meat on the bottom of the pan as then the food will taste bitter. I do this in three batches and, for the final one, I add the trimmed bones to colour up too. Once all the meat and bones are browned off, stick them aside.

Add a good amount of olive oil to the same pot, bring it up to temperature, and add your diced onion. When the onion first hits the pan they will release their natural water. At this stage, while the onions are still wet, you want to use a wooden spoon to scrape off any of the browned meat sticking to the bottom; it's just free flavour that's going to give you real depth. Add a big pinch of salt to your onions and cook until deep, dark and sweet. Don't rush this – stews and slow braises are all about layering flavour and onions cooked in lamb fat are delicious.

Once the onions are cooked, stir in your sliced carrots and slowly cook them down to add sweetness. Return your lamb to the pan along with the peas. Everything you add will cause the temperature to drop so allow the pan to come back up to heat before adding the next ingredient as this way you get the most flavour. You can't just add everything to a pot and expect, by some miracle, for it to be delicious at the end. Listen for that hiss from the pan as this means it's frying again. Also, try to layer your seasoning. Seasoning all your food at the very end is super boring, but if you layer the seasoning as you go, the flavour stands out more.

So where was I? Cool, lamb and peas are back in, we're back to the frying sound, now add your tomato purée. Stir that through everything in the pan and fry for about 5 minutes. Tomato purée is full of natural sugars and I like to cook it to the point just before the sugars caramelize and stick to the bottom of your pan. Add the canned tomatoes in next. I buy whole tomatoes, rinse off the tomatoey water they're sat in and just squeeze them in with my hands. Again, season, bring the tomatoes up to the boil, and then add five cans' worth of boiling water. Bring the liquid in the pan to the boil, lower the heat a tad (not completely to low unless you want to eat it in like 6 hours), and simmer gently for 1½ hours.

Half-way through cooking, the watery tomatoes will have cooked out, so taste it now and check for seasoning – you need to be able to taste the salt. If you can and you're happy where it's at flavour-wise; you're on the home stretch. Let it continue cooking until the lamb has no resistance when you pinch it between your fingers. Serve with rice, yogurt and loads of bread for the table.

Bamya

I absolutely love okra. That is all.

SERVES 4

1.8kg/4lb whole chicken, jointed
olive oil
700g/1lb 9oz okra
vegetable oil, for frying
500g/1lb 2oz white onions,
   finely diced
1 tbsp tomato purée
2 x 400g/14oz cans chopped
   tomatoes
sea salt and black pepper

Preheat the oven to 170°C fan/190°C/375°F/gas mark 5.

Season and seal all your pieces of chicken in a little olive oil in a heavy-based frying pan. We just want a nice caramel colour all over. Once all the chicken is sealed, remove from the pan and set aside.

Using the same pan, add 2.5cm (1in) vegetable oil and shallow-fry the okra all on all sides until it starts to soften and crisp. Do this in batches so the oil temperature doesn't drop and the okra fries evenly. When all the okra is fried, discard the oil and transfer the fries to a plate lined with kitchen paper to soak up any excess oil.

In a new pan, add a little glug of olive oil. Fry the onion with a pinch of salt over a medium heat for 10 minutes until soft and translucent. Once the onion is soft and sweet, add the tomato purée and gently fry off for a couple of minutes. Add the canned tomatoes and cook slowly over a medium heat until the mixture comes to the boil.

Place the okra, sealed chicken and the tomato sauce in a roasting tray, season with salt and pepper and bake in the oven for 45 minutes or until the chicken is cook through and some of the okra has popped open.

Tarhana

The last couple times I've been to Cyprus, my dad's sister, Gulseren, has always made us this soup to celebrate our arrival. Now, it sounds weird when you explain it as dried wheat, yogurt and helim soup but it's an absolute classic, and whenever mum makes it at home it always reminds me of my *hala*.

Now, packet helim is fine – the type you can get in a supermarket. However, if you take a little trip to Green Lanes, you'll find the helim in big plastic containers of brine, straight from Cyprus. For me, that's what helim is. That's the stuff I'd watch my aunties make as a kid – it's saltier, harder and has more of a squeak to it.

SERVES 4

1.9 litres/3½ pints Chicken Stock
300g/10½oz tarhana
200g/7oz helim, cubed

For the smashed parsley
15g/½oz flat-leaf parsley
½ garlic clove
1 tbsp red wine vinegar
50ml/2fl oz olive oil
sea salt

Start off by bringing your stock to the boil and don't worry about seasoning it as the tarhana is salty. Drop in your tarhana and allow it to blip for 15 minutes. The tarhana will suck up the stock and start to thicken. We want the soup to be a loose porridge consistency. Stick the soup over a low heat and let it bubble away while we fry off the helim.

Pan-fry the helim until it's golden on all sides, then drop it into the soup and let it simmer for another 5 minutes, just so the helim can completely soften.

It's not traditional, but I like to make to make a little smashed parsley to go on top.

Pick the parsley leaves off the stalks and stick them in a pestle and mortar with the garlic and a little salt to help break everything down. Once the mixture is completely smooth, add the red wine vinegar and stir. Finish with the olive oil.

Divide the soup between four bowls and add a little spoonful of the green stuff to each one. Jobs a good 'un.

Cyprus Chips

Listen, I know that this is just a recipe for frying chips, but honestly Cyprus potatoes make the best chips. They have a lower sugar content, are full of starch and sit in-between crispy and a little golden brown. They are another thing that's served with a lot of Cypriot dishes and my auntie will often make black-eyed peas, potato koftes, a couple salads and a huge bowl of Cyprus chips. Good chips aren't about cooking them four times in four different oils and then stacking them like a shit game of Jenga and charging someone £9. Chips are comfort, poor-people food and really can be eaten with anything. Also, while I'm talking about how our potatoes are superior, if you can find Cyprus potatoes, then there's a good chance that the same shop will sell Turkish ketchup – get the spicy one and, trust me, it will taste like almost every holiday you've ever been on.

SERVES 4

8 Cyprus potatoes
1 litre/1¾ pints vegetable oil
sea salt

Peel the potatoes, then slice each potato into four lengthways and cut each slice into little potato batons. I don't like uniform chips; I like it when you get one that's a little weird looking. Also, the weirdly shaped ones go crisp because they have more corners.

Heat the oil in a large cast-iron pan until it's at 160°C/325°F. It's important to use a cast-iron pan because it retains the heat while batch-cooking.

Fry the chips off a handful at a time – we're looking for the chips to just cook through but without any colour. Let the chips sit on a clean cloth, towel or in a wide sieve to drain and cool slightly. Once all the chips are blanched, get the oil up to 180°C/350°F and fry them for about 3 minutes until golden brown.

Drain the cooked chips and, while still hot, put them into a metal bowl with a generous crack of sea salt.

The best chips you'll eat. Promise.

Makarna Bulli

(Poached Chicken Spaghetti)

Possibily the most celebrated Cypriot dish. Midweek, weekend, if you're well, if you're ill, there's nothing more Cypriot than *bulli*. I'm not going to lie, coming home and asking Mum what was for dinner and hearing 'bulli' was soul destroying. I've been a food snob from a young age and my mum was just taught to literally boil a chicken for hours until it was fucked. So here's how I do it; and although Kamil was sceptical about my processes, he thought it was very 'eatable'.

SERVES 4

1 quantity Chicken Stock
    (see page 16)
1 chicken, weighing 1.8kg/4lb
olive oil
220g/8oz helim cheese
7g/¼oz dried mint
500g/1lb 2oz zita pasta or any
    other long pasta with a hole in
    the middle
chilli flakes or Turkish ketchup
    (optional)
sea salt and black pepper

So the chicken stock on page 16 is what we're using to poach our chicken – we don't want to jeopardize the cooking of the chicken just to make the pasta taste better. Bring the chicken stock to the boil in a large pan, add two big pinches of salt and your chicken. Make sure your chicken is fully covered; if it isn't, just top it up with a little water. Gently poach the chicken for 25 minutes – just slow, casual bubbles, nothing too hard.

Once the chicken is poached, pull it out and let it sit for 10 minutes. After it's sat and it's not as hot as the sun, break your chicken down but try not to lose the skin as we are going to crisp it up in a pan later. Start by cutting off the legs and separating the thighs. Take off the breasts. The chicken will be ever so slightly undercooked and floppy but trust me, you're good.

Heat a frying pan with a little glug of olive oil. Pat the chicken dry and season both sides with salt and pepper. Gently the fry the chicken over a medium heat – we want the skin to go super golden and crispy and to gently warm the meat through.

In the same stock we boiled the chicken in, we are gonna boil the pasta. Taste the stock and make sure it is salty enough to boil the pasta, then cook for 8 minutes.

While the pasta boils, grate the helim into a bowl and mix in the dried mint.

Line up the bowls you're gonna serve in and add a little of the helim mix to the bottom. Carve the chicken breast and leave the thighs on the bone and stick them on a separate plate.

In the pan the chicken was crisping in we are going to finish our pasta like the Italians would. Leave the excess fat in the pan, add your cooked pasta, a glug of the stock and a good splash of olive oil. We want the pasta and sauce to be wet to melt the helim. Give it a little toss over the heat so the olive oil emulsifies the stock. Put the pasta and sauce into the serving bowls with the helim in the bottom. Scatter plenty of helim and mint over the top, plus any liquor left in the frying pan. I like to add a pinch of chilli flakes over the top of mine or some spicy Turkish ketchup – it sounds rank but it bangs, promise.

Seftali
Kebab

Cypriot food is very rich, but not pretentious, olive oil-heavy and served course after course. Food is celebration to us; aunts always cook in huge numbers and live off an old saying: 'What if we have unexpected guests?' Food in Cyprus, like the people, isn't very complicated – everyone lives off their land and nine times out of ten there's a butcher in the family. In my family, my grandad was the village butcher and he also had an abattoir. Well, I say abattoir – you'd take a live goat or sheep to his house, and he'd kill it in the garden. No long ting. My dad used to tell me, 'My fada one time, punch de cow and the cow fell on the floor.' He'd chuckle, fag in one hand, legs crossed gazing up into the sky. Although my dad has lived in London for thirty odd years, I know there's a part of him that desperately wants chickens running around our garden.

The Turkish word *seftali* means peach, but there isn't any fruit in this recipe. I think it's just a way of describing how sweet and juicy the kebabs are. Someone told me this dish was first made by a man called 'chef Ali', hence the name. Probably bullshit. Seftali kebab is always on the menu at a Cypriot BBQ. The Turks on the north side don't really eat much sausage and, if we do, it's often in an artificial casing or one that's just shite. Seftali is wrapped in caul fat (lamb's abdominal membrane, mmmmm yummy), which you can get frozen in most foreign butchers. Defrost it and rinse well, then give it a wash with a few lemons or a good glug of vinegar. It will get the arse-y smell out of your kitchen. I'm not selling these well I know, but they are so easy and delicious, you should really give them a go. Fuck a basic banger.

SERVES 10

1 packet of frozen caul fat (about 3kg/6lb 8oz)
juice of 2 lemons, plus extra to serve
1 white onion (approx. 155g/5½oz)
60g/2¼oz flat-leaf parsley, chopped, plus extra to serve
1 lamb shoulder, minced (get your butcher to do this – none of that supermarket fatless stuff)
15g/½oz pul biber (see page 16)
a big pinch of sea salt and black pepper

To serve
pitta breads
white onion, thinly sliced
tomato, sliced

Wash your caul fat under the cold/hot tap to help it defrost. Once it's defrosted, stick it in a bowl with the lemon juice and give it a proper wash. Scrub bits of the caul fat together as if you were getting a stain out of a T-shirt. Set it aside for 1 hour and move on to the filling.

Light your BBQ following the instructions on pages 18–19.

Chop your onion down to as fine as you can get it – don't put it in the blender, you'll bruise the onion and release its juice. Roughly chop your parsley; I like it quite chunky as it looks good in the mix. Add your onion and parsley to the mince. Go in with your pul biber next and season generously with salt and pepper. Take a bit of your mix and taste it – you can cook it if you really want, but raw lamb isn't gonna hurt you, I promise.

Take your caul fat and cut it into 15cm/6in rectangular pieces. Take 30g/1oz of your meat mix and shape it into a sausage. Lay out a piece of caul fat, stick your mince in and roll. You don't want a thick layer of caul fat; it should only be one layer. Make sure you tuck in the sides as well – we want to keep it compact. Roll as many as you can. You should get about 30–35 sausages from the mix.

Stick them on your grill on a steady heat, nothing too hot – we want to cook these slowly. Basically, what we are doing is slowly rendering the caul fat. The idea is that the fat melts back into the sausage, keeping it dangerously moist. Cook the sausages for about 20 minutes, turning continuously to achieve that golden colour. They're traditionally served in a piping hot pitta bread, with thinly sliced white onions, a handful of parsley and a few slices of tomato. Assemble, add a good crack of salt and a big squeeze of lemon juice. LOVE!

Barbun
(Fried Red Mullet)

My dad will cook himself whatever he likes, he doesn't care if everyone isn't up for it. I recently came home to a house smelling of fried fish and Dad on the sofa watching something on Facebook with the dog licking his fingers. 'Why does it smell like fish in here?' I asked. He replied, 'I don't know', so obviously I opened the bin to investigate. The man had fried and eaten eight red mullet on his own. Must have been payday. Dad doesn't really know how to cook – he can fry fish and grill meat, both with very little salt. But whatever makes you happy, innit. Large up Kamil.

Also, make sure you are buying red mullet. Don't let them sell you goat fish. They look exactly the same but are nowhere near as tasty.

SERVES 2

4 red mullet, gutted and scaled
1.5 litres/2¾ pints olive oil
500g/1lb 2oz plain flour
500g/1lb 2oz coarse cornmeal
sea salt and black pepper

To serve
bread
½ white onion
lemon wedges

Rinse your red mullet, making sure there's no blood or scales. Red mullet turns fast, so cook them the same day you buy 'em.

Heat the oil in large saucepan. We're not deep-frying the fish, just a little shallow-fry job. On a deep plate, mix together the flour and cornmeal and season heavily with salt and pepper.

Dry off the fish completely, then dip them in the flour mix. Heat the oil to 180°C /350°F and shallow-fry the fish for 4 minutes on each side. Don't overcrowd the pan, we need the oil to stay hot to ensure the fish is crispy. Drain the cooked fish on a piece of kitchen paper and season with salt and a squeeze of lemon juice. My dad eats these with his hands with a piece of old bread and half an onion.

Firinda Makarna

I guess this is our version of a lasagne. It's a celebration dish – if it's someone's birthday or the week you touch down in Cyprus to see family, at least two of the aunties will have made it. For me, this is comfort – it's home.

If you do have any leftovers, leave them in the tray and reheat in the oven the next day so the bits of pasta go crispy. Those are the bits to fight over.

SERVES 8

olive oil
1.2kg/2lb 11oz minced beef
2 large white onions, diced
2 bunches of flat-leaf parsley,
    roughly chopped (stalks and all)
20g/¾oz crushed black
    peppercorns
1.2kg/2lb 11oz bucatini
350g/12oz butter
800g/1lb 12oz helim, grated
200g/7oz plain flour
2 litres/3½ pints full-fat milk
120g/4½oz Parmesan cheese,
    grated
150g/5½oz kasar peyniri or other
    stringy cheese, grated
a grating of fresh nutmeg
4 eggs
sea salt

Preheat the oven to 170°C fan/190°C/375°F/gas mark 5.

First off, heat up a heavy frying pan with a glug of oil. Add the minced beef and fry for 10 minutes until it releases all of its moisture. The moisture will evaporate, and the beef will start to fry again. Fry the mince until it's just starting to crisp, then add the onions and fry with the beef until soft. Add in the chopped parsley and season generously with salt and the cracked black pepper. Transfer the cooked beef mixture to a deep baking tray. That's our bottom layer.

Cook the pasta in heavily salted water according to the packet instructions. Drain the pasta and cool it down in a colander under cold running water. Lay the cold pasta on top of the meat – it doesn't really need to be neat, but you need to make sure that it's evenly stacked. Squash 100g/3½oz of the butter over the cooked pasta just for a little extra naughtiness. Scatter 200g/7oz of the helim over the top, giving it a little mix so that it gets down to the bottom layer too.

The top is just a good old-fashioned béchamel sauce, heavy on the cheese. Melt the remaining 250g/9oz butter until it just starts to foam, then add the flour and cook gently. Using a whisk, make sure the mixture is moving. We basically want to cook out the flour so that our béchamel is smooth and thick. Add the milk, a quarter at a time; the first quarter will get completely sucked up by the roux. Keep stirring. Add the remaining milk when the mixture is getting too thick. Add in all the grated cheese and whisk until melted. Grate in the nutmeg, take the béchamel off the heat and whip in the eggs. Season your béchamel with salt so the cheese sings.

Pour the béchamel over the pasta and fill it to the top. Bake for 45 minutes–1 hour until the top is brown and crisp. Remove from the oven and let it sit in the tray for at least 15 minutes before portioning it.

I like to eat mine with a massive whack of spicy ketchup; a little hat tilt to the Cypriot cousins. LOVE x

Badadez Kebab

This is the equivalent of a Cypriot Sunday roast. In Cyprus, most houses have an outdoor wood-fired oven and this dish cooks slowly for hours with burning olive-tree logs gently smouldering. I don't have one (I wish I did); if you do, defo do this in there; if not, you'll have to stick to good old-fashioned indoor oven-cooking like me.

Now, Cypriots don't really care about cooking chickens beautifully. They'd just put this all in a tray and stick it in the oven for hours, but as no one wants to eat sawdust chicken, I've stripped the recipe back and tried to get it to a point where whoever gets the breast can actually enjoy it.

SERVES 4

1 chicken, weighing 1.8kg/4lb
olive oil, for drizzling
a bunch of thyme
800g/1lb 12oz round shallots, peeled
1.5kg/3lb 5oz Cyprus potatoes,
    peeled and quartered lengthways
500g/1lb 2oz sweet pointed peppers
320g/11½oz long green Turkish
    peppers
a good glug of olive oil
3–4 tbsp tomato purée
sea salt and black pepper

To serve
good-quality olive oil
chopped flat-leaf parsley
zest of 1 lemon
rice
Turkish yogurt
nice bread

Preheat the oven to 160°C fan/180°C/350°F/gas mark 4.

Start by breaking down your chicken. Cut off the legs, then split the thighs and the legs. Take off the wings with a little breast. Cut out the backbone and cut the breasts into three equal pieces on the bone. Keep the breast on the bone – that's our little safety blanket to stop our chicken drying out, plus the bone adds to the flavour.

Stick your chicken in a bowl, give it a good glug of olive oil, season with salt and pepper and a bunch of thyme. Don't really worry about marinating, just dress it.

Heat a heavy-based frying pan over a medium heat with a good glug of olive oil and seal your chicken. Make sure you brown your chicken on all sides to build flavour but don't burn the thyme. Once the chicken is sealed, stick it on a plate and set aside.

Now, it's pretty much just stick everything in a roasting tray. Add the shallots and potatoes first, then slice the pointed sweet peppers into three, remove the seeds and add to the mix. The green Turkish peppers can just go in whole. Add the vegetable oil and season everything heavily with salt and pepper.

Stir the tomato purée in to 850ml/3¼ cups boiling water, then add to the mix. Add the chicken we sealed off earlier, leaving the breast behind for later. Place the tray in the oven and cook for 2 hours. We want the potatoes to suck up all the flavour.

After 2 hours, add the breast meat over the top. Don't mix it through as you want to avoid breaking up the potatoes. Turn the oven up to 210°C fan/230°C/450°F/gas mark 8 and cook for 15 minutes. The chicken breast will cook through, and your potatoes will crisp around the edges.

Pull it out of the oven and let everything rest for 10 minutes because otherwise it will 100% burn your entire mouth. I like to finish mine with a good glug of olive oil, chopped parsley and lemon zest. Serve with rice, yogurt and bread. Happy Sunday x

Fasulye

Another Cypriot summer classic. Green beans are in season almost all year round in Cyprus. I actually don't like them when they make my teeth squeak; it weirds me out. However, this dish is cooked low and slow so the beans become sweet and fall apart. No squeaky beans over here.

SERVES 6

1.3kg/3lb leg of lamb, bone in
1kg/2lb 4oz green beans, trimmed top and
    bottom
2 white onions, finely diced
4 garlic cloves, sliced
2 tbsp tomato purée
2 x 400g/14oz cans whole tomatoes
sea salt and black pepper

To serve
bulgur rice
Turkish yogurt

Now, if you're getting the meat from the butchers, which I think you should, ask them to take the meat off the bone for you, but keep the bone (it's full of flavour and the marrow from the bone will make the dish silky).

Cut the lamb into 5cm/2in dice and leave the fat on (I don't bother trimming it down). When sealing meat, I find the fat just adds to the overall flavour. Season it heavily with salt and pepper.

Heat a high-sided frying pan with a good amount of olive oil over a high heat. When the oil just starts to smoke, add in half of your lamb and seal the meat on all sides. You want a nice deep colour and, if you overcrowd the pan, you wont be able to achieve this. Please don't just throw all the lamb in at the same time as then you've fucked it from the beginning. Be patient; do it in stages. For the last round of sealing, add the bone and let it colour up.

Transfer the sealed meat to a plate and set aside. Don't clean your pan but add the onion to the same oil you browned your lamb in. Fry off your onions for a good 15 minutes on a medium heat. They'll go from watery and translucent to catching a little bit of colour and turning sweet. Season with a heavy crack of salt. When making dishes as simple as this, it's all about cooking everything to the right stage. Once the onions have taken on some colour, add in the sliced garlic. Turn the heat down a little and fry for at least 5 minutes. We don't want any colour on the garlic, we just want it to be nice and fragrant. Add in the tomato purée next and fry until it starts to catch on the bottom of the pan. Add in the

green beans and give it all a mix, making sure that the green beans have bean covered in the sauce. Add the lamb next and allow everything to heat up again. Add in the tomatoes (I always use whole San Marzano tomatoes; they're expensive but have the best flavour). Again, season the mix with a little salt to start building layers of seasoning. Fill up one of the empty tomato cans with boiling water and add that in. Season once more with salt and loads of freshly cracked black pepper.

Cook the stew on a medium heat for a good 2 hours until the beans have fallen apart and the lamb is tender enough to pull apart. I like to serve with bulgur rice and a big whack of Turkish yogurt.

Manti

When making this, the smell in the air reminded me of my nene (Kamil's mum). I'd often walk into the kitchen in Cyprus and she would be chopping, rolling or peeling something with her leathery-looking but somehow delicately soft hands. The horizon just peeking out of the kitchen window and the smell of fresh dough in the air. The kindest woman, whose only goal in life was to make sure everyone was fed, happy and comfortable. This one is for my nene.

SERVES 4

For the dough

1.2kg/2lb 11oz 00 flour, plus extra
    for dusting
1 egg

For the filling

250g/9oz lamb mince
10g/¼oz flat-leaf parsley, finely
    chopped
sea salt and black pepper

For the yogurt sauce

400g/14oz yogurt
3 garlic cloves
sea salt

To garnish

75g/2¾oz butter
1 tbsp pul biber (see page 16)
pinch of dried mint

Start off with the dough – I made mine in a mixer. Add the egg to the flour, start to mix and slowly add 530ml/19fl oz water. Once it comes together evenly and there's no flour left in the mixing bowl, tip the dough out on to your work surface and knead for 5 minutes until smooth. It's quite a stiff dough but, once it's smooth, wrap it in clingfilm and chill in the fridge for 1 hour.

While the dough is chilling, make the filling. Place the lamb mince in a bowl, mix in the parsley and season generously with salt and pepper.

When the dough is ready for rolling, lightly flour the work surface (don't go too heavy as it will make shaping the dumplings harder). Split the dough into three pieces. Take a piece and roll out into a rough square – we need to get it pretty thin and you should be able to see your fingers through the dough. Repeat this with each piece and portion the dough into 4cm/1½in squares.

Now fill each square with about ¼ teaspoon of filling. Honestly, this is a bit of a long process but if you get everyone together to help, you'll smash it. Before this book, the last time I made manti was years ago and I got my mum and sister to help.

I find shaping the dumplings easier if you're holding them in your hand. Also my back is super bad, so hunching over the worktop to roll

just under 250 dumplings is back-breaking. You want the little square of dough to be the points of a compass when you look down on it. So bring south to north and pinch the two points together. Next, bring the eastern point to the top two. When folding the edges you'll be left with two straight edges on that side; pinch those together, making sure it's sealed. Do the same on the other side. Basically, do that 250 times and you're done.

The yogurt sauce is pretty straightforward. Mix the yogurt and garlic with 3 tbsp water in a bowl.

The last bit of prep you need to do is melt the butter until it's brown. You want to take it to the point where it smells like butterscotch, making sure it's golden and not burnt. Add the pul biber and take it off the heat. The pul biber will make the butter foam, so make sure you do this in a fairly deep saucepan.

Boil the little dumplings in salted water for about 3 minutes, until they start to float to the top and turn translucent.

Strain the water and spoon the dumplings out into a bowl (ou need about 30 per portion). Dollop over the yogurt – you want about 2 tablespoons yogurt per portion. Drizzle over the pul biber butter and finish with a pinch of dried mint. Turkish pasta mate.

THE
GRILL

Kamil's Chicken

This recipe has been in the family since Dad was a kid; it's had many variations, from squashing in a kiwi to tenderize the meat to marinating it overnight with yogurt. I think that me and Kamil have finally got it to a point where it's at its best and, to be honest, that's happened from just simplifying and stripping it down.

It's super important to get yourself a brilliant chicken for this – don't get me wrong, of course you can make it with a supermarket chicken, but if you can get your hands on a big, beautiful, organic bird, it's just gonna be better. Growing up, this marinade always went on little cubes of chicken breast or on bone-in, skin-on thighs. The more I cooked on the BBQ and understood temperature, the more I used spatchcocked chickens. Whole chickens aren't the easiest to cook, but if you have a go, it pays off hugely. BBQ'ing a chicken low and slow is a game-changer – it allows you to slowly build flavour and great colour.

SERVES 4

For the chicken

2.2kg/5lb organic, free-range
    chicken, spatchcocked
3 tbsp kirimizi toz biber (see
    page 16, or a really good
    sweet paprika)
3 tbsp pul biber (see page 16)
1 garlic bulb, finely grated
190ml/7fl oz vegetable oil
juice of 2 lemons
sea salt

For the dressed herbs

20g/¾oz coriander
20g/¾oz flat-leaf parsley
15g/½oz mint
1 green chilli
2 tbsp pomegranate molasses
20ml/4 tsp good-quality
    olive oil

**For the yogurt and cumin
tomatoes**

1 tsp cumin seeds
430g/15oz cherry tomatoes
1 large garlic clove
150g/5½oz strained yogurt (look
    for the stuff called *suzme* in
    Turkish supermarkets)
20ml/4 tsp good-quality
    olive oil
sea salt and black pepper

lavash or other flatbread,
    to serve

Place all the ingredients for the chicken, except the chicken, in a bowl and mix together. Use the marinade to cover your chicken, then leave to marinate for 1–8 hours. The marinating time isn't super important as we're going to double dip our chicken while it's cooking.

Heat your BBQ to a 3 count (see pages 18–19), take your chicken out of the marinade, hold it above the bowl and allow the extra oil to drip back in. Season your chicken generously all over, then place it on the BBQ, carcass-side down. The reason we are going carcass-side down first is to check out the BBQ temperature and to give ourselves a little bit of a safety net. The marinade is oil-heavy in order to create that kebab-shop smoke, BUT if we were to go skin-side down first and our grill is too hot, we've ruined the skin and it's pointless after that.

I like to turn my chicken regularly, every 2–3 minutes at the beginning. The temperature of the charcoal will drop once you're cooking so, when it first goes on, it's vital that we continuously move and turn the chicken so we don't get any burnt spots. After about 15 minutes, slowly building smoke and colour, we can turn less regularly. Now, when our chicken is gently hissing away, have a poke and prod with a finger and feel the meat; it should feel slightly tighter but still have a waterbed-like fluidity. Check the temperature of your chicken using a thermopen – I reckon you'll be at about 24–34°C/75–93°F.

Now it's time to double-dip your chicken in the marinade, again

allowing the excess oil to drip off before putting it back on the BBQ. You can repeat this until the marinade is finished, or give the chicken a little baste with a pastry brush until you're all out of marinade. Continue cooking the chicken for about 15 minutes.

OK, so guys in lab coats will tell you that 'Your chicken must have a core temperature of at least 75°C/167°F', but those people don't cook at home and probably also don't care about eating a piece of meat at its absolute prime. Take your chicken to 61–62°C/141–144°F and then leave it to rest for about 15 minutes. The internal temperature will creep up to about 65–69°C/149–156°F.

While the meat is resting, roughly pick the coriander and parsley leaves – a little stalk is good as that's where the flavour's at, plus it also adds another texture. Strip the mint leaves from the stalks. Put all the herbs in heavily-iced water. This will give the herbs a crispness and shock them back to freshness. Leave them in the iced water for a good 10 minutes. Once the herbs have crisped, take 'em out and dry them completely; if you don't dry them thoroughly, the dressing won't stick and will just stay in the bottom of your bowl.

Slice your chilli super fine – just everyday rounds, nothing special. Put it in a bowl with the rest of the dressed herbs ingredients and mix together.

To make the yogurt and cumin tomatoes, start by toasting and crushing your cumin seeds.

Dry-toast the cumin seeds in a small pan over a medium heat until they turn golden brown and fragrant, then transfer to a pestle and mortar and crush into a powder. Slice all your tomatoes in half; I like to do this horizontally as I think they look prettier – it doesn't add anything to flavour, it's just attention to detail. Add the cumin, then grate in the garlic. Mix in your yogurt next and season with a big crack of salt and a little pepper. Add your olive oil and stir it in slowly. The oil and the yogurt won't mix so it will all look separate, but we want that. We want the hum of garlic, freshness from the tomatoes, acidity from the yogurt and pepperiness from the olive oil.

Flash your rested meat on the BBQ to warm through and then carve. When you first cut this chicken, the brown meat may look pink but, trust me, it's cooked; I've cooked chickens 'dangerously' ever since I met Barnaby Benbow at Fifteen, years ago, and haven't died since.

This dish gets better if you just stick the meat, herbs and tomato in some warm lavash, roll it up all together and smash it.

Jerk Pork

Bro, I live in Edmonton, the shithole bordering Tottenham where jerk shops outnumber any other takeaways. My brother's a jerk chicken fiend and, when he's not listening to Ibrahim Tatlises, he's daggering to Vybz, Aidonia and Mavado. This one's for Arif. My actual brother.

Side note – while shooting this, the heat split the crowd. If you're not really a fan of hot hot, go for three Scotch bonnets. It's not all about the heat though, as Scotch bonnets give you a fruitiness that I really like.

SERVES 4

4 x 250g/9oz pork neck steaks
vegetable oil

For the marinade
a bunch of coriander
a bunch of spring onions
5 Scotch bonnet chillies (or 3 for less heat)
25g/1oz thyme sprigs
35g/1¼oz fresh ginger, peeled
6 garlic cloves, peeled
2 tsp allspice
1 tsp ground cinnamon
1 whole nutmeg, grated
70ml/2½fl oz dark soy sauce
2 tbsp dark brown sugar
80ml/2¾fl oz tropical fruit juice
1 tbsp sea salt and black pepper

For the jerk BBQ sauce
leftover marinade
65ml/2¼fl oz tropical fruit juice
170ml/6fl oz BBQ sauce
1 tbsp red wine vinegar

Start by chopping all your marinade ingredients into more manageable pieces – you can't just stick everything in a blender and expect it to work. Not unless you've got a proper industrial ting, those are sick. Anyway, back to you and your blender. Start with the coriander, stalks and all, spring onions, Scotch bonnets, thyme, ginger and garlic. Blend all together until it's almost a paste, then add your spices and blend again. Then go in with the soy sauce, sugar, fruit juice and salt and pepper. Blend once more. I always make a fair bit of jerk marinade and turn the remainder into a little jerk sauce afterwards. We'll get into that soon. Cover your meat in the marinade and marinate for a minimum of overnight and a maximum of three days. The longer the better.

Set up the BBQ to a 3 count (see pages 18–19). Season the steaks with salt and a little vegetable oil, then grill for 3–4 minutes a side, turning them 45 degrees every 45 seconds. By the time you've done a full turn it's time to flip. Do the same on the other side, then allow the steaks to rest.

Fry off the leftover marinade in a little veg oil for about 4 minutes – 1 minute to cook away any of the rawness and 2–3 minutes to create a little bit of colour. Add the fruit juice and cook until reduced, then add the BBQ sauce next and bring it to the boil. Add the vinegar and allow to cool. Dress the steaks with the BBQ sauce and allow to rest for 5 minutes before serving.

Hake, Romesco and Grelots

Romesco is a sauce that originates in Catalonia in Spain. It's a popular side dish amongst the fishermen and traditionally made from just roasted tomatoes, garlic and hazelnuts, roasted in the oven. I like mine with grilled cherry tomatoes and red corno peppers for that smokiness and a cheeky bump of paprika.

SERVES 2

700g/1lb 9 oz sweet pointed
   peppers
200g/7oz cherry tomatoes
4 garlic cloves, skin on
olive oil
150g/5½oz hazelnuts
1 tsp sweet paprika
1 tbsp sherry vinegar
8 Grelot onions, peeled
juice of 1 lemon, plus wedges to
   serve
1 tsp chopped chives
vegetable oil
2 x 300g/10½oz hake fillets,
   skinned
sea salt

Start off by getting your grill to a 3 count (see pages 18–19) and preheat the oven to 140°C fan/160°C/325°F/gas mark 3.

I don't bother seasoning my peppers, I just stick them straight on the grill. Build the colour slowly, turning them constantly. You have to treat them with the same amount of respect as you would a big expensive steak. Blister your tomatoes and garlic cloves in a metal sieve, then season with a little glug of olive and some salt. We're adding oil to the tomatoes because we don't want to blacken them. When the tomatoes and garlic are soft to the touch, stick them in a warm spot on the grill so they don't go cold. Once the peppers have gone completely soft and the skin pulls away easy, stick them in a bowl and cover with clingfilm. The clingfilm will catch the moisture from the steam in the peppers and make peeling them easier. Leave them in the bowl for at least 10 minutes.

While the peppers steam and the tomatoes keep warm, roast your hazelnuts. Spread the hazelnuts out evenly on a baking tray. Zig-zag olive oil over the top, making sure each hazelnut has a little bit. Crack over some sea salt and give the nuts a little shake to pick up any salt left on the tray. Roast in the oven for about 40 minutes or until they've turned a nice deep brown. Nothing too dark, just like the first three days of your holiday suntan.

Peel all the peppers, removing all the seeds, and stick them in a pestle and mortar. Add your blistered tomatoes and roasted garlic (peeled) and give them a good smash. You want to smash them pretty smooth. Add your roasted hazelnuts and break them down. At this point you're looking for a dry red-pesto consistency. Add the paprika and sherry vinegar to the party. Add a big crack of salt and taste – it should be deep, sweet, smoky, salty and finish with a little acidity. Stir through enough olive oil so you can spoon it and it holds its shape – we don't want to drown out all the flavours we've spent time building.

While the grill is still hot, dress the Grelot onions with olive oil and salt. Always go olive oil first so that the salt sticks to your ingredient when cooking over fire. Grill the onions until they've

built a nice colour all over and are soft to the touch, then take them off the grill and peel off the first layer of burnt skin. Season with olive oil, salt and lemon juice and then add your chives. I just do this on my chopping board – no point getting another bowl dirty. That's all the outside stuff done.

Heat a frying pan over a medium heat with a little splash of veg oil. You should all invest in a good non-stick pan for cooking fish. It will save your arse a million times. While your oil is heating, season your fish with salt on every side, not just top and bottom. Lay your fish in the pan away from you, removed-skin-side down. Once it's in, leave it. We don't want a super hard fry, keep it on medium. The fish will slowly change colour

the more it cooks – keep it removed-skin-side down for a good 5 minutes. I always cook fish 80% on one side – it gives you enough time to build that beautiful golden exterior. Have a little peek using a palette knife and see how your fish is cooking – don't turn the fish over to look, just give it a little lift. Turn the fish over and let it cook on the other side for 1 minute. Just 1 minute. Leave the fish in the pan and turn the heat off – the fish will continue to cook slowly in the residual heat.

Put the dressed Grelots on the plate, fish on top and slightly off-centre, then top with a big spoonful of romesco. Zig-zag some olive oil over the top and serve with a wedge of lemon. Summer holidays mate. *Gracias por favor.*

Scallops

This recipe is dedicated to the BBQ award-winning, curly-haired, food-she-touches-turns-to-gold Milli Taylor. The first time we cooked together at mine, Mills brought over scallops. She asked me if I had ever cooked them in their shells, straight in the coals. Not gonna lie, I was mad sceptical. Mills heated the scallop shells up, seasoned the flesh lightly with salt and just let them fry in the shells with a touch of olive oil. She was onto a winner. Mills' dad, Dave, was one of many who pushed me into going solo. Told me to chase my dreams and leave the job I was in behind when shit got problematic. Dave kinda reminded me of me in a way; clumsy, tall, enjoyed chat and could throw out random bits of information on any topic. We had a special friendship. We may even have held hands one night, on our way back from a curry.

Get the scallops in the shell and ask your fishmonger for large or XLs – you may need to pre-order. I got mine from Steve Hatt on Essex Road. BIG UP STEVE!

I could eat all eight but you could probably bring two friends if you really wanted.

SERVES 3 (OR 2 OR 1 HAS)

8 large or extra-large
   scallops
25g/1oz flat-leaf parsley
1 garlic clove
good-quality olive oil
a couple of pinches of
   smoked hot paprika
zest and juice of 1 lemon
sea salt

Light your BBQ, following the instructions on pages 18–19.

To take the scallops out of their shells, hold the curved shell pointing towards you. The flat side of the shell is where the scallop is most attached and the corner of the shell is the weakest point: you'll see there's a little notch you can slip your palette knife in. Once the palette knife is in, give it a little twist to pry it open a little. Without touching the scallop, bring the palette knife to the top and slide it in so it sits horizontally across the shell. Slide the palette knife down until you can feel you are touching the scallop's flesh. Angle the knife against the shell. You need to make sure you are touching the shell at all times, otherwise you'll cut the scallop in half. Scrape the scallop off the flat shell all the way down. Now you can fully open the shell and the flat side should be completely clean. (You could probably ask your monger to do this for you, but you must keep the shells to cook them in.)

Using a spoon and the same technique, scrape the scallop out of the curved shell.

Push your thumb through the frilly bit attached to the scallop and run your thumb around it to separate it from the meat. You'll notice there's a little bit of flesh that's a different texture to the rest of the scallop. Peel that off vertically and everything will peel away. Do this to all of the scallops. Rinse them clean, dry them and ensure they are the right way up. You want the elongated side to be the side facing you when you season them, with the flat side on the bottom. Rinse the curved shells and dry them, ready for the BBQ.

Quickly chop the parsley and garlic and mix them together. The scallops will cook pretty fast so it's best if we've that done beforehand.

Stick the shells directly in the charcoal and they'll slowly start to blacken. The charcoal has to be pretty hot for this to work, otherwise the scallops will stick to the shell.

Once the scallops have taken on colour, add a tiny splash of olive oil to each one and season your scallops with a good amount of salt on one side. Place the seasoned side down into the shell. Season the other side while the flat side cooks. Once you've put the scallops down, don't touch them. Just keep an eye on them – the rims will start to take on colour and will smell great. Give them about 1½ minutes to cook on the first side, then flip them and cook for 30 seconds.

Add a little splash of olive oil to each scallop and throw in the garlic and parsley mix you made earlier and cook for about 20 seconds. Take the scallops out of the fire, sprinkle with a pinch of paprika and a couple strikes of lemon zest. Then give each scallop a little squeeze of lemon juice. Smash 'em.

Adana Kebab

There's defo an art to this one and attention to detail is needed when cutting the meat and not just whacking it through a mincer. Just so you guys all know, this is probably the only recipe in the book that gave me loads of trouble. However, the satisfaction of getting it right a day before my deadline made this long stretch a little more bearable. I hope you all get it right first time and feel as good as I did!

The first couple times I tried to make this, I fucked about with working out ratios and percentages like I was in a year 8 maths lesson. Fuck all that. Back in the day, the kebab boys wouldn't have bothered and I'm a fully-fledged, seasoned, hairy-armed kebab boy now. So just ask your butcher for a boned lamb shoulder weighing 740g (1lb 10oz), with the glands removed and the fat and skin on; the fucking lot.

MAKES 5 SKEWERS

740g/1lb 10oz boned lamb
    shoulder
1 tbsp pul biber (see page 16)
1 tbsp kirmizi toz biber
    (see page 16)
1 tbsp sea salt
200g/7oz sweet pointed
    peppers, super finely chopped

Slice the lamb as thin as you can get it, then cube it up super small. It doesn't have to be uniform – we are gonna run our big chopper over it after this, so it's just to make our lives easier. Chill the finely chopped meat for 1 hour as we are essentially gonna chop the shit out of it and if the meat warms up, the fat will start to melt, and you'll have more a burger consistency.

Traditionally, in the motherland, adana would be made with a *zirh* – a big traditional rocking chopper. You can get them here and I picked one up from a cash and carry locally, but it's achievable without one. You just need a big sharp knife that you can get your weight behind. Chop through the meat until it starts to resemble mince, you want there to be flecks of meat and fat, but we don't want the mix to become smooth and emulsify, otherwise it won't stick to our skewers. You should be able to ball the mix up in your hand and it should stick together. If the mix doesn't do this, keep chopping until it does. It will, I promise. When you eventually get there, after about 10 minutes of chopping, add the spices, salt and peppers and chop them through, folding the mix every now and again. Don't mix it with your hands at all. Once you have an even tinge of red through your meat and you can bring it together without it falling apart, stick it in the fridge for at least 1 hour, as the mix has to be cold to get it on the skewers.

You need to buy the right skewers for this – the flat ones, 2.5cm/1in or so thick with a pointed tip, as it won't work any other way. Portion the mix into 180g/6oz balls, trying not to mess about with it too much. They're not all gonna weigh exactly the same, so just weigh the first one and use that as a reference. Mould your meat mix into a fat sausage no bigger than the palm of your hand. Stick the skewer through the bottom end until 7.5cm/3in of the top of your skewer is exposed. Slowly stretch your mix down your skewer, pinching the meat on to the skewer and working your way down until you have a kofte that's about 25cm/10in long. Once all the meat is on the skewers and looks pretty, you want to cook it straight away.

Set your charcoal up to a 3 count (see pages 18–19). The first 5 minutes of cooking the adana is the most important – we don't want to build the colour too quickly – we are going to slowly grill our skewers for about 15 minutes, turning constantly. The more the meat warms up, the more the fat will drip to create smoke. By the end of the cook we want a nice golden kofte, smoky from the fat and still retaining the moisture. If you want to be really cheeky and you're confident the meat won't fall off the skewers, just before pulling them off, take one off the grill and press all the fatty flavour into a flatbread and lay that bread back across the skewers while they cook for a naughty meat–bread situation.

Grilled Octopus

I've got memories of being in Cyprus in the school summer holiday, watching my nan repeatedly smashing an octopus in the sink and thinking to myself, 'What the actual fuck is this woman doing?' I remember it being really tough and really salty but my dad and grandad both loving it.

This is a proper Cypriot classic – grilled octopus, beans cooked in the octopus stock (my doings), raw onion, bread and a couple pickled chillies. I guess this one is for me. Tastes. Like. Home.

SERVES 4

2 kg/4lb 8oz octopus, defrosted
   (I doubt you'll find a fresh one)
30g/1oz table salt
7g/⅛oz black peppercorns
14g/½oz fennel seeds
12g/¼oz coriander seeds
60g/2¼oz flat-leaf parsley stalks,
   plus 20g/¾oz to garnish
2 lemons, 1 sliced and juice of 1
1 carrot, roughly chopped
5 celery sticks, roughly chopped
olive oil, for cooking
good-quality olive oil, for
   finishing
sprinkling of flowering oregano
sea salt

For the beans
550g/1lb 4oz fresh beans, such as
   borlotti or coco de paimpol,
   podded (see page 16)
olive oil
500g/1lb 2oz onions, finely
   chopped
3 garlic cloves, finely sliced
2 tbsp tomato purée
440g/15½oz fresh tomatoes,
   grated

To serve
pickled chillies
white onion, quartered

Defrost the octopus under running water. Don't bother smashing it in the sink – that stuff doesn't work, I promise. Frozen octopus' are already prepped, so there's no guts or anything, just make sure you rinse out the head in case they've missed anything.

While the octopus is defrosting, let's get the stock sorted. Fill the biggest pan you have with water. You're gonna need at least 6 litres/10½ pints. Add the salt, whole peppercorns, fennel seeds, coriander seeds, parsley stalks, sliced lemon, carrot and celery. Let the stock come up to the boil. Although I don't do the whole smashing in the sink thing, I do do the three dunks. Honestly, I don't really even know if this works, but if it ain't broke, don't fix it, innit. Holding the hollow octopus head, dunk the octopus in the boiling stock from the tip of the tentacles up to just under the head where all the tentacles meet. Quick dunks though – an in-and-out job, not holding it in. After three dunks, drop the octopus in and cover with a plate and a weight (I use my pestle and mortar). Make sure the entire octopus is under water so that it cooks evenly. Simmer the octopus for 25 minutes. Once the octopus is cooked, pull it out and leave it on a tray to cool.

Light your BBQ before you get the beans on (see pages 18–19).

Sieve the stock of all the little bits and bobs and save 2 litres/3½ pints for the beans. Freeze the rest for the next time you're cooking octo or beans. Stick the beans in a saucepan, then cover with water and bring to the boil. Boil the beans in just plain water for a good 5 minutes, skimming off any gunk that rises to the top. Discard the water and keep the beans.

In the same pan, add a good glug of olive oil. Add the finely chopped onions and sweat down for 20–25 minutes until sweet. Go in with the garlic and gently fry until soft. Add the tomato purée next and fry for a couple of minutes until it starts to smell sweet, then add the grated tomatoes and bring to the boil. Once boiling, add the beans and cover with the octopus stock. Bring to the boil, then reduce the heat and simmer for about 50 minutes until the beans are soft and the stock has reduced. If your beans cook quicker, a little trick is to squash one quarter of them against the side of the pan. The starch will thicken the sauce. Always season beans after they're cooked; if you season them at the beginning, the skins will become tough and you'll be cooking them for hours.

Grilling the octopus is pretty easy. Make sure your octopus is dry and then rub a bit of oil over the tentacles and season heavily with salt. You want to grill the octopus over a 2 count (see pages 18–19) otherwise it will stick. The best way to do this is to put it on the grill and don't move it until the tentacles are crispy and brown. Once brown, then you can turn them. They'll take about 6–7 minutes a side. Once the tentacles are browned, stick them on a chopping board. Finely chop the parsley and scatter over the tentacles, squeeze over the lemon juice, drizzle a good amount of olive oil and sprinkle with a good bit of flowering oregano.

I serve the octopus and beans on the same plate with a couple pickled chillies and a quarter of a raw white onion. Old school classic.

Lamb Chops

This recipe means a little more to me than the rest of them. Salsa rossa is great on everything – BBQ meats, roasts, up against some veg, and I particularly like it in a cheese sandwich. This is the first recipe I ever shot with George for Jamie Oliver's YouTube. I guess this is the birth of Sunday Sessions. I tried to make something that tasted like a kebab-shop dish but a little better. Big up George each and every time. SUNDAY SESSIONS FOR LIFE!!!

SERVES 4

12 lamb chops
1 lemon, cut into slices
Confit Garlic (see page 42)
1 tsp flowering oregano
flatbreads, to serve

For the labneh
900g/2lb full-fat yogurt (look for *suzme* or *koy*)
zest and juice of 2 limes
4 garlic cloves
2 tbsp caster sugar
15g/½oz sea salt

For the salsa rossa
2 x 400g/14oz cans whole tomatoes, washed
4 red chillies
6 garlic cloves
olive oil, for drizzling
2 tbsp fennel seeds, toasted and crushed
1 tbsp coriander seeds, toasted and crushed
a pinch of saffron (optional if you're a millionaire)
50g/1¾ oz runny honey
50ml/2fl oz white wine vinegar
sea salt

For the onion salad
1 red onion
25g/1oz flat-leaf parsley
2 pinches of sumac

The labneh needs to hang overnight, so let's start with that. Put the yogurt in a bowl and add the lime zest and juice. Grate in the garlic, add the sugar and salt and mix well. The juice from the limes will loosen up the yogurt but it will firm up once we've hung it. I don't often have cheesecloth or muslin knocking about, so I normally run to the cornershop and buy a couple of pairs of cheap tights. The mix will fit into one leg of the tights, but if you want it done quicker, split the mix in half and use both legs. I don't bother hanging it in the fridge. I'll make it in the evening and hang it on the washing line. You need to make sure that the tights are free-hanging as gravity is going to help with the moisture. Worst-case scenario, line a sieve with a clean cloth and add the yogurt, keeping it over a bowl in the fridge overnight.

You can make the salsa rossa in the oven but I like to do mine on the drumbecue. It's a BBQ in an oil drum so allows for smoking. I don't really smoke according to different temperatures, I just light the BBQ, then let the temp come down to a 3 count (see pages 18–19), throw in a couple of logs, let them catch fire and then move them away from the fire to smoulder. Close the lid and let it do its thing.

Add the tomatoes, chillies and garlic to a roasting tray with a good glug of olive oil and a crack of salt. If you're doing this in the oven, do the same thing and roast it at 210°C fan/230°C/450°F/gas mark 8 until the chillies start to colour and the liquid has cooked away from the tomatoes. This way, they start to become sweet and we also want a deep, rich colour on our mix. Add your crushed spices next and fold them through, then return the tray to the oven for a further 5 minutes. Mix the honey and vinegar together. Take the tray out the oven and put it on your hob with the gas ring on underneath. Bring it up to temperature and, once it starts to fry, crush everything together with a potato masher – it doesn't have to be completely smooth. Add in the honey mixture, with the heat on high, and deglaze the tray, scraping any bits that have stuck to the bottom. Transfer the cooked salsa to a bowl and cover with olive oil. It will keep in the fridge for a couple of weeks under oil.

If you're cooking the salsa rossa on the BBQ, do everything the same but you won't have to put it over the gas ring. The heat from the charcoal will do the reducing for you. For best results, I'd defo go BBQ – smoky, sweet, spicy and acidic is what we're looking for.

The lamb chops we're not really gonna do much to. We've got all sorts of flavours going on and we just want the lamb to be delicious as it is. Leave the fat on your chops, just ask your butcher to French-trim them. Don't flatten them like they do in kebab shops. Season the lamb just with salt. Get your BBQ to a 4 count (see pages 18–19) and line your chops up all together, fat-side down. The fat will slowly melt, giving you smoke clouds of flavour. Render the fat out until the fat side is golden, dancing and half the size it was originally, then rejig your charcoal so that you've got a solid 3 count. We want heat to build a bark on the outside of the chops. Grill the lamb chops for 2 minutes on each side. I give mine a quarter turn every 30 seconds. Fuck grill marks, we just want the entire exterior of our lamb to be crispy and delicious and still have a juicy pink centre. Flip them and repeat.

Make a cheeky little resting tray using the lemon slices, confit garlic and oregano. Rest the lamb in that for at least 5 minutes. We are going to flash-cook the lamb again, so it doesn't matter if it chills in there for a little longer. While the lamb rests, slice the red onion as thin as you can get it. It's easiest to do this on a mandoline but a sharp knife and some practice will do. Pick in the parsley leaves, add your sumac, salt and a good crack of pepper and mix with your hands.

Flash-cook your lamb for a couple minutes on each side. While the lamb is warming, throw a couple flatbreads on the grill. Once they're hot, add a good dollop of the labneh and put them on a plate. Swirl the cooked lamb chops in the resting tray and put them on top of the bread and labneh. Spoon over the salsa rossa. Plonk the onion salad on the side. Then, the only thing missing is a glass of raki and a couple of grilled chillies.

Grilled Fish

Honestly, I eat more grilled fish and seafood than anything else – squid, scallops, whole fish or fillets. I find grilling a piece of fish beautifully is more satisfying than cooking anything else. Crispy skin, soft flaky flesh, and all I really want alongside is a wedge of lemon, crack of salt and a drizzle of nice olive oil.

Get your fishmonger to gut and scale your fish. Also ask for them to break the bloodline along the spine. I can't stress the importance of buying a super fresh line-caught bass. Yes, I know they're about £29 a kilo, but it was caught sustainably, the fishermen got their bit and so did the fishmonger. Don't do this with a supermarket fish or a farmed fish, there's literally no point. If you want to eat a beautiful piece of fish and have that holiday nostalgia, you have to get something line-caught, not a trout that swims around in a tight box with chlamydia. (True story – google it.)

SERVES 4

1 sea bass, weighing 600–800g/1lb 5oz–1lb 12oz
olive oil, for cooking
good-quality olive oil, for finishing
1 lemon (Amalfi if you can, see page 16)
sea salt

The fish prep is pretty simple. When you get your fish home, rinse it under the tap. The blood line runs along both sides of the spine – you'll see it, it's like congealed blood. Make sure you wash that away completely. If the blood stays in, we can end up with a bitter fish and we're after the freshest, buttery fish we can get. The fish will have been sat in its own juices in the bag and the enzymes can start to break the fish down – we want to keep it as fresh as possible. Dry the fish completely, and be dramatic with it; no half-arsed bullshit – make sure the fish is DRY. Water + oil + BBQ = stuck skin and a big waste of time.

Rub the fish with a splash of olive oil on both sides. Imagine you are putting on suntan lotion, you don't want loads, you don't want it to be dripping off you before you get in the pool, but you want enough to know it's there. Season the fish heavily with salt, from the cheeks to the very end of the flesh on the tail.

You need a pretty hot grill for cooking fish as the intense heat, together with the oil, creates a barrier on the fish skin, allowing it to go crispy and not stick to the bars.

Place your fish on the grill horizontally, with the belly of the fish facing you, over about a high 2 count (see pages 18–19). Now, it's quite a big fish, so make sure you are at a 2 count the entire length of the fish. We don't want any uneven hot spots – we want all the fish to cook at the same heat. Once the fish is on the grill, we are not going to move it until the skin is crisp. The reason we lay the fish belly towards us is because we can see the flesh on the belly slowly cook and it will come in handy when flipping. After about 5 minutes, you'll notice the flesh inside the belly start to turn opaque, and the very edge of the belly start to go golden and crispy. Now we can have a prod and poke. I usually do this with a fork. Starting at the head end of the fish, I'll slip the fork

through the grill and see if I can lift the fish off the grills with no resistance; if you can't, don't try and force it, as long as the temperature is right and you dried the fish beforehand, you'll be fine. It's all about patience.

Once the fish comes away from the grill with no resistance, that's your cue to turn it. The fish is telling you: 'Turn me over, you've cooked me enough on this side'. I don't really ever touch the flesh or use a skewer to feel if the meat is cooked as once the skin is crispy on both sides, I know it's cooked. Flip the fish in one swift motion – when the skin's crisp it's less likely to fall apart. Cook for the same amount of time on the other side. Again, wait for the cues, let the fish tell you – you're just there to look after it. Lift the fish on to a big plate and let it rest for a couple of minutes.

Open up the fish like a pair of curtains along the spine, flip the belly-side out one way and the fatter side the other. Gently lift the head and the clean spine should follow. You know your fish is cooked perfectly if there's still a little shade of pink in the bones. This takes a few times to get right but works with every piece of fish you'll ever grill. I like to re-season my fish once the spine's out, so go in with a little crack of salt, a squeeze of lemon and a good glug of olive oil.

Personally, I don't even bother with a fork. I watched my dad as a kid open up his fish, season it and dress it, all with a hot pitta bread off the grill tucked away in his palm so he could still use his fingers. Dad also taught us as kids to eat fish with our front teeth. He would explain 'use your front teeth so you don't find bones' and then go on about how my uncle had a tuna bone in his throat the size of his middle finger.

Summertime, ladies and gentlemen. Grilled fish and lemons.

Rib-eye Steak and Salsa Verde

SERVES 2

500g/1lb 2oz rib-eye steak (Basque or
    Galician are my favourites)
olive oil
sea salt and black pepper

For the salsa verde
20g/¾oz mint
20g/¾oz tarragon
50g/1¾oz flat-leaf parsley
50g/1¾oz basil
1 garlic clove, peeled
2 anchovy fillets
135g/4¾oz capers
50g/1¾oz Dijon mustard
40ml/3 tbsp red wine vine vinegar
200ml/7fl oz pomace oil
    (see page 17)
140ml/4½floz nice peppery olive oil

Honestly, I don't even want to think about how many times I've made this. I spent a lot of my career as the guy on the grill in restaurants like Rotorino, Palatino, Craft London, the lot.

I first made salsa verde with Santos at Fifteen. If we were ever doing staff lunch, an event or were on a team-building trip, Santi would always have two little gastros, one full of fresh, acidic, deep and peppery salsa verde and one with a bright red chilli oil. It just makes sense when you've got a beautiful fatty, rich steak, screaming 'I need freshness, vibrancy and acid'.

I've eaten a lot of steaks in my time, mostly during service. I can say, hand on heart, every steak I ever cooked I ate a slice. Quality control, innit? Someone's gotta do it. However, I'll never go to a restaurant and order steak as I feel that, with top-quality butchers popping up everywhere and the pandemic forcing everyone to do home deliveries, a great 'restaurant-quality steak' is something you can cook at home. Also, I don't believe in making salsa verde for just one dish, so you'll end up with a good portion of leftovers, which is great on fish, roast potatoes, in sandwiches or with your Sunday roast.

Right, let's talk salsa verde. You need a sharp knife; if you do this in a blender, I'll judge you. Wash and dry all your herbs, don't be lazy and, finally, I want everything super finely chopped.

Pick all of your herbs so it's just the leaves, I know there's flavour in the stalks, but I don't really like them in salsa verde. The easiest way to get the herb chopping consistent is to chop them individually. The herbs themselves have different structures and different amounts of water, so we want to take care of them.

I bunch the herbs together and slice them finely, almost like you are julienning them. This makes it easier to run your knife over them and chop them super finely. We need a sharp knife so we don't bruise our herbs. We want to chop them but not allow them to piss flavour into the chopping board. It's like chopping an onion; if you use a blunt knife to cut an onion, you'll cry double the amount (you're breaking its structure by forcing a blunt object into it).

Once all your herbs are chopped, stick them in a bowl.

Paste the garlic and anchovy by running a knife over them, adding a little crack of sea salt and then using the flat side of your knife to scrape them until you've got a smooth paste. Add the paste to your herbs.

Chop all your capers the same size as your herbs and add them with the mustard. Add the red wine vinegar and mix before adding both oils. The red wine vinegar will help the herbs stay a vibrant green. The salsa verde can be made a day in advance and live in the fridge for a good three days, providing the oil is covering the top. The longer you leave it in the fridge, the more it will start to mellow. If you are using it a couple days after making it, add another splash of red wine vinegar to bring it back to life. However, for best results, eat it on the same day without it going in the fridge.

I always cook steak at room temperature. It cuts your cooking time in half and lets you do the index finger–thumb trick (if you use your finger to feel the fleshy part of your thumb, that's how a steak cooked to medium-rare should feel). You can't do that with a fridge-cold steak as it goes from hard raw meat to bouncy and almost feels like working backwards.

Get your grill to a 3 count (see pages 18–19), rub your steak with a little olive oil and a give it a good coating of salt on both sides and all the way round.

Stick the steak on the BBQ; I don't really care about bar marks; the idea is to create a crust all the way round the steak. Bar marks are for visuals, and I find the only part of a steak with bar marks on that tastes like BBQ are the bar marks. What's the point?

I turn my steak 15 degrees every minute or so until I've done a full circle. Have a little peek underneath and you should have built a nice crust all the way round. Flip and do the same. Give the meat a little poke and the meat should feel soft and bounce back. The tighter the meat gets, the more it's cooked. Cooking a rib-eye anything after medium is just a waste of money; steaks are a luxury, so why would you cook all the flavour out? Just trust me, go medium-rare.

Once you've got a little tightness and a good bouncy feel, rest your steak on a plate away from the BBQ until it comes down to room temp.

Flash your steak for 3 minutes on each side, just to warm it through, then carve against the grain and stick it on a plate. Pour any resting juices over the top. Give the steak a little crack of pepper and a top up of salt. Be super generous with the salsa verde; I like a big tablespoon and a little nice peppery olive oil over the top. You won't need to order a steak in a restaurant again. Promise.

Kebab-Shop Sis

I think I'd go as far as saying lamb is the king of BBQ. Clouds of lamb-flavoured smoke, farmy flavour in the best possible way, crispy bits of dancing fat almost golden in colour. Normally I'd just put lamb on skewers with a big whack of salt and keep it super traditional, but I know you guys all want to get that little kebab-shop experience at home. I think the success of sis all comes from a good-quality piece of lamb to start with – the better it is, the less you have to faff about with marinades. A good piece of lamb – whether it be neck, saddle or, in this case, shoulder – a long rest, a crack of salt and some bread and I'm home, man.

MAKES 4 SKEWERS

600g/1lb 5oz lamb shoulder
10g/¼oz kirimizi toz biber
  (see page 17)
10g/¼oz pul biber
  (see page 16)
10g/¼oz minced garlic
120ml/4fl oz vegetable oil

Basically, this is about half a lamb shoulder – ask your butcher to remove the little glands as you can't eat those. Cut the meat with the grain, into finger-width lengths. Keep the fat on as it's going to help with the flavour. Lean cuts of meat don't do well over fire, so we want a few fatty bits that we can distribute amongst our skewers. Now, cutting against the grain, cut the lamb into thumb-sized squares, about 4cm/1½in, then place in a bowl, mix with the remaining ingredients and set to one side.

I don't really marinate lamb for a long time. Light your BBQ (see pages 18–19) and, by the time the charcoal is up to temperature and ready to cook on, the lamb will have sat in the flavours for long enough.

Let's talk skewers – first off, bamboo skewers are shit and shouldn't be used over fire. I don't care how long you soak them, they'll always burn, and the handles will get too hot to handle. I like the square-cut skewers with the coiled ends. The ones about 38cm/15in long are best for my BBQ; if you don't have a huge BBQ, you can find smaller ones in most Middle Eastern supermarkets.

Skewering meat isn't just about putting it on a stick; there's an art to it. You ever skewered something and it's heavier on one side or won't sit the way you want it to? Well, I'm here to give you the down-low on how to stop that shit happening, yo!

Basically, you need to skewer against the grain of the meat – the grain is the way in which the fibres run in the meat and is super visible in red meat. So, you want your grain to be running horizontally and the skewers to go through vertically. Now, as you push the skewers through the meat, you need to pinch the meat pretty tight. Basically you're contracting the muscle so the meat stays where you skewered it. Try to put

any leaner pieces of meat back to back, so the skewer is two lean pieces and one fatty piece, repeating until you've got about 12 pieces of meat on each skewer.

You want your BBQ at a steady 4 count (see pages 18–19). Knock the charcoal about so you don't have any spots that are too hot. We want the fat from the lamb and the oil to provide little droplets that will then create smoke and give us all the flavour possible. I turn my skewers every minute or so – we want to cook them evenly and slowly caramelize the outside for a little texture. If you leave them too long on one side, you'll burn the spices and go from crispy and delicious to dark and burnt. *No bueno.*

To check the cooking, pick up a skewer and give a piece of meat in the middle a little pinch – it should feel tight but still have a little bounce. I rest my lamb on the skewers like I would any other meat.

In my house and most of Cyprus, lamb sis is served in a stupidly hot pitta bread, with chopped onions, tomatoes, parsley and lemon juice. You can do whatever you like, but for me that is the way to eat it.

Kebab-Shop Onions

Before becoming a chef, I'd obviously eaten in my fair share of kebab shops and this is one of those things that I'll always order. I remember being in a kebab shop in the ends and asking the chef how to make it and he was pretty reluctant to give his secrets away. However, I'm not a cock and this is hardly a 'secret' recipe. The 'secret' is basically turnip juice. Game-changing, I know. You can get this in almost every Turkish supermarket or cornershop and it's normally in the fridge with the drinks. If boss man has only got the big bottles, just buy it and drink it with a couple glasses of raki like a proper Turk. Next time you light the BBQ, you have to make this.

SERVES 4

2 red onions, cut into quarters
olive oil, for drizzling
5 dark green, long Turkish peppers
4 tbsp aci salgam (spicy turnip juice)
80ml/2¾fl oz pomegranate molasses
10g/¼oz picked flat-leaf parsley
1 tsp sumac
sea salt

Give the onions a little splash of olive oil and a big crack of salt. Skewer them so that are all sat horizontally – this will give you more control when turning them. Do the same with the peppers – you'll need to put two skewers through the peppers, one at the top and one near the bottom, as otherwise they'll wilt over the charcoal and you'll have unevenly cooked bits.

Get your BBQ up to about a 4 count (see pages 18–19). We want to cook the onions soft and slow, building the sweetness and cooking them through gently. This will take about 20 minutes. I always stick these on at the start of a BBQ. I'll pull a little charcoal over to one side and let the onions slowly do their thing while I'm messing about with other stuff. The edges of the onion will slowly crispy and go sweet while the rest of the onion steams under the heat of the charcoal. When the onions are slowly starting to feel soft to the touch, stick your

peppers on. We don't really need to give the peppers our full attention, just blacken them slowly on each side and allow them to steam.

Once everything is soft and delicious, you're good to go. Take the onions off the skewers and slice off the root that's holding them all together. Separate each petal, discarding the first outer layer as those ones are always tough – you don't want to be the person to get that one. Peel the roasted peppers and cut into about 5cm/2in chunks.

Place your onions and peppers in a bowl with a little crack of salt. Dress the mix with the turnip juice and pomegranate molasses. Give everything a good mix up so that the dressing has a chance to coat everything. Throw in the picked parsley and sumac. It's great in pittas with roasted meats but also, once all the good stuff is gone, the little dressing in the bottom is great for dipping bread into.

Pastirma Sandwich

Pastirma is a cypriot sausage, made from loosely ground lamb and spiced with pul biber and garlic. It's almost a Turkish chorizo, if you will. We normally eat them for breakfast with eggs or as something hot to put in a sandwich.

This isn't really a recipe as such. When we were kids, Dad would always stick pastirma on the grill first and then eat it in a crispy bit of BBQ'd pitta as he cooked. Growing up, Mum and my brother Arif weren't into garlic – 'it makes me smell / makes the house smell' – so pastirma was only really ever allowed to be cooked outside on the BBQ. Sometimes, I'd cook one in the microwave when Mum was at work and then later I'd swear I hadn't. Anyway, when I started to take BBQ Sundays on tour (and by on tour, I mean to Robert's house) with the mandem, I introduced Robert to what he now calls his 'BBQ starter'. And almost every BBQ since, he's started the same way.

MAKES 6 SANDWICHES

6 pastirma
2 Bull's heart tomato
Turkish pide (the big oval bread you get in Turkish bakeries with the diamond pattern)
Turkish ketchup – spicy or sweet stuff, it's up to you (optional, but I would)

The casing on a pastirma isn't edible, run your knife down the middle just to break the skin. The casing should peel away easy if the pastirma is fresh, though if it doesn't it's not a big deal. Run the pastirma under the cold tap. The skin will tighten, making it easier to peel. Once peeled, cut the sausage in half lengthways so it opens up. I like to find a little spot on the BBQ that's at a 4 count (see pages 18–19) and just let them tick away.

Pastirma has a high fat content so they create a lot of smoke. You can cook them over a high heat but you have to be careful as they have a tendency to create a fire ball. Place the pastirma on the grill with the outside facing downwards. Let the pastirma cook gently, allowing the fat to drip to create smoke. I try to cook them 70% on one side (usually, about 5 minutes). Flipping them, you'll lose a bit of the oil but it's fine. Cook them inside-down for a further 3 minutes.

Cut the bread and let it slowly warm through on the grill. Once the bread is nice and warm, add in the pastirma and give it a good squeeze. You want the bread to soak up all that oil to make your sandwich even better. Add in a couple slices of tomato, squirt in a good amount of ketchup. Welcome to the family.

ITALY

Rich Egg Yolk Pasta Dough

Everyone's got a bloody pasta dough recipe, so here's mine. I prefer egg yolk pasta as I find that it tastes better – you get that bite, deep colour and a fuller flavour.

MAKES 1.2KG/2LB 12OZ

700g/1lb 9oz 00 flour
24 free-range egg yolks
2 whole eggs

Turn your flour on to a work surface and make a well in the middle that will hold all of your eggs. Add your yolks and whole eggs into the middle of your flour. Using your fingers, slowly stir the eggs round, bringing in a little more flour from the edges each time. Continue to do this until it's too hard to stir.

Using a pastry scraper, fold the rest of your flour in and chop it through, mixing wet into dry until it forms a rough dough. If you've got a wooden chopping board, knead your pasta dough on the wood to draw out the moisture. I knead pasta for 20 minutes. Not joking. Like four songs on your playlist. You want to knead the dough until it's smooth and leathery.

Wrap in clingfilm and chill for no less than an hour.

Semolina Pasta Dough

Semolina doughs are eaten throughout the south of Italy and used to make pasta shapes like pici, cavatelli and orecchiette. All the good stuff.

MAKES 1.5KG/3LB 5OZ

500g/1lb 2oz 00 flour
500g/1lb 2oz fine semolina
2 eggs

I start this dough in a bowl. Add the flour and semolina to a bowl. Weigh the eggs (cracked), then add enough water so that the mixture weighs 550g/1lb 4oz, then beat together.

Add the egg and water mixture to the flour and mix it in with your hands. Knead in the bowl until it forms a dough. Tip the dough on to a work surface with all the bits in the bottom of the bowl. Knead the dough on the work surface for 15 minutes until completely smooth.

Wrap in clingfilm and chill for no less than an hour.

Cacio e Pepe

So 'cacio e pepe' just means cheese and black pepper. It's probably the easiest pasta recipe you'll make in your life. Traditionally from Rome and served with tonnarelli, which is a square-cut spaghetti, it works with all pasta shapes, but I like mine with spaghetti. You need a fine microplane grater for this recipe – it's a must!

SERVES 2

50g/1¾oz Parmesan cheese
75g/2¾oz Pecorino cheese
50g/1¾oz butter
5g/⅛oz freshly cracked black
    peppercorns
250g/9oz fresh spaghetti
salt

As in every other pasta recipe, start off by bringing a pan of salted water up to a rolling boil.

Grate the two cheeses into individual bowls.

The key to making silky smooth cacio e pepe is building the butter emulsion. In a pan, gently melt the butter until it starts to foam, then add your black pepper and let the butter gently toast. You'll see the butter start to change colour and the pepper fumes will build in the kitchen and take in all the butter flavour. Cook the pasta in the pan of boiling water for a minute less than the packet instructions.

Turn the heat up to high under the pan with the butter and black pepper. Add a big ladle of pasta cooking water to the butter, shaking the pan in a circular motion as you do so.

So, scientifically, mixing fat into liquid shouldn't work. It's like a rainbow-coloured puddle in a garage where the oil has a high density and sits on top of the water. However, with heat and agitation we can manipulate the compounds of each component. In normal people terms, we need to keep the heat high and keep swishing the watery buttery mix around the pan until it starts to thicken.

Add your cooked pasta to the butter, still over a high heat, allowing any water off the pasta into the pan. (Don't ever drain your pasta into a colander over a sink.) When the pasta has soaked up the butter, add another ladle of pasta water. Now the emulsion is established, we are going to stir in the cheese with a wooden spoon.

Stir in the Parmesan in two handfuls at a time. The Parmesan will melt pretty quickly and thicken the sauce. Once all the Parmesan is in, add half a ladle of pasta water and slowly feed in the pecorino over a high heat, stirring continuously. Once all the Pecorino has melted, add a little pasta water and stir – we want the sauce to be thick but still have fluidity, we don't want it to be fatty and just solidify on the pasta when it touches the plate.

Plate up two equal portions, spooning over any leftover cheese sauce. It should be peppery enough as it is. If you want a little more, go ahead. But you've been warned!

Crab Tagliatelle

Honestly, crab, pasta, garlic and chilli. It doesn't get much better. Save this one for when the sun is beaming. Take the book to the beach and set up as if it was a Sunday Session.

SERVES 2

olive oil
2 garlic cloves, thinly sliced
2 red chillies, finely diced
160ml/5½fl oz Chicken Stock (see page 16)
440g/15½oz fresh tagliatelle
220g/8oz picked crab meat
25g/1oz flat-leaf parsley, finely chopped
zest and juice of 1 lemon
nice peppery olive oil, for drizzling
sea salt

Add a glug of olive oil to a pan with the garlic and chilli and fry them gently over a medium heat. Once the garlic is soft, translucent and sweet, add the chicken stock and crank up the heat to high to bring to the boil.

The fresh tagliatelle doesn't need long to cook if you've made it fresh that day. Bring a pan of salted water up to a rolling boil. Add the pasta and cook for 1 minute; if you made the pasta a day before, cook it for 2 minutes.

Add the cooked pasta to the boiling chicken stock; the pasta will suck up half of the stock almost straight away. Add your picked crab meat and stir it through. Then add the parsley, lemon zest and juice. Add a good glug of nice peppery olive oil and a pinch of salt. Toss the pasta until the chicken stock starts to thicken. The liquid consistency should go from loose to thick after a good few tosses.

Plate up and enjoy.

Vongole

I reckon this is my all-time favourite pasta – I might even go as far as saying it would be my death row starter. My love for vongole comes from its pure simplicity and how powerful it is, using just five ingredients.

<u>SERVES 2</u>

800g/1lb 12oz clams
250g/9oz linguine
olive oil
2 red chillies, deseeded and finely sliced
4 garlic cloves, thinly sliced
150g/5½oz cherry tomatoes, halved
130ml/4fl oz white wine
20g/¾oz flat-leaf parsley, finely chopped
good-quality olive oil, for drizzling
sea salt and ground black pepper

Buy your clams from the fishmonger – they can sit in the fridge but don't leave them in the bag the fishmonger gives you them in. I rinse my clams in salty water so they open up and let out any sand or grit in their shells. If you're going to put them back in the fridge to use later, leave them in an uncovered container.

Start off by bringing a pan of heavily salted water up to a rolling boil. Cook the linguine until al dente as there's a lot of sauce in vongole that we want our pasta to suck up and cling on to.

Add a good glug of olive oil to a large frying pan, then add your chillies and garlic. Cook over a medium heat until the chillies and garlic are slowly starting to fry, then turn the heat to low and gently fry until the garlic is translucent and the chillies change the colour of the oil to ever-so-slightly red. Don't get any colour on your base; you're flavouring the oil that's going to cling to your pasta when we're finishing the dish.

Add your clams to the pan and put the heat on full whack. Stir the clams through the chillies and garlic and, when you can hear that everything is frying hard and fast again, add the tomatoes and then the white wine. Stick a lid on the pan, keep the heat high and cook for 2–3 minutes until all the clams have opened. Get rid of any clams that haven't opened as they were dead before they went in the pan.

You should have a good amount of powerful juice in the pan, so season the cooked clams now. Add the al dente linguine, then go in with a generous amount of olive oil and continue to cook the pasta over a high heat. When the pasta is rapidly boiling, start to toss it – if you can't toss it, then just stir it pretty fast with a wooden spoon.

The point of tossing your pasta is that we're trying to make two ingredients that don't normally mix, mix. So in this case we have added olive oil to clam juices and are breaking down the molecules that stop fat and water emulsifying through heat and manipulation. Honestly, it's not as boring as it sounds. When you first start tossing the pasta, you'll see that it's all still pretty liquid. However, the more you toss the pasta, the tighter and thicker the liquid will become. I boil my sauce once, give the pan about 10–15 tosses, put it back over a high heat to boil the sauce, then add my parsley. Toss again 10–15 times and then serve.

Spinach and Ricotta Mezzelune

This tomato sauce is super basic, but you have to source some really good-quality jarred San Marzano tomatoes. I always buy them whole as I feel that chopped tomatoes cook too fast and can give you a floury mouthfeel.

SERVES 3

½ quantity Rich Egg Yolk Pasta
    Dough (see page 120)
Semolina, for dusting (optional)
15 basil leaves
sea salt

For the filling
500g/1lb 2oz spinach
400g/14oz ricotta
a grating of fresh nutmeg
6g/⅛oz sea salt
1g freshly ground black pepper
40g/1½oz Parmesan cheese,
    grated, plus extra to serve
juice of ½ lemon

For tomato sauce
8 garlic cloves
100ml olive oil, plus extra to serve
3 x 240g/8½oz each jars San
    Marzano tomatoes, drained and
    washed
10g/¼oz sea salt

Let's start off with making the tomato sauce. We've all seen that infamous scene in *Goodfellas* where Paulie and the boys end up in prison, right? Razor slowly slicing through garlic? Anyway, we're doing that. Stick on Bobby Darin's 'Beyond the Sea'. Shit, light a cigar if you want. Slice the garlic cloves in half and remove the root. Slice the garlic as fine as you can get it – slicing the garlic gives you more control. Have you ever made something where you mince the garlic? It goes in a hot pan, you get beautiful garlic smells in the kitchen and then, before you know it, some of it is dark, bitter and burned. Cooking is about control and understanding how ingredients work; what you can do to make your life easier and build the best flavour.

Add the olive oil to a saucepan over a medium heat, then add the garlic. When the garlic starts to gently fry, lower the heat a little. We want the oil to suck up all the garlic flavour so we want to cook it pretty slowly, and make sure it doesn't colour. The garlic will slowly start to release all of its sugars and clump together. Add your tomatoes and turn the heat up to medium. Break the tomatoes down with a wooden spoon and season with the salt. You'll notice the juice from the tomatoes and the oil won't mix; we're going to cook all the tomato juice out until we are left with a deep red, intense tomato sauce. Cook it gently, slowly blipping away for about 45 minutes.

For the filling, blanch the spinach in heavily salted water. You want to be able to pinch the stalks of the spinach and break it apart in your hands. Then shock the spinach in ice-cold water to stop it cooking. Once the spinach is cold, squeeze all the moisture out using a tea towel and then finely chop – you don't want any long stray bits in your filling; you want it to be smooth and consistent. Mix the spinach with the rest of the filling ingredients, then stick it in a piping bag and chill in the fridge.

Roll the pasta down to level 2 (see page 147). Then, using a mug as a guide, press out 16–20 flat discs. Mezzelune is probably the easiest pasta shape you can make and a great one to do with kids if you have them/the patience. Pipe about ½ tablespoon filling into the middle of the pasta, depending on the size of your discs. I line the discs up and stick the filling in, then fold them one by one. I find the easiest way to fold them is to pick them up, resting two fingers underneath the pasta and filling, then use your other hand to push the filling down and into the corner. Work from one side to the other, pinching the remaining edges of pasta together and making sure to squash the air out at the same time. There you go. Little pasta moons.

Now, the important bit is bringing it all together. Make sure you have a big enough pan of water up to the boil; you want the pasta to boil with enough freedom to cook evenly – you don't want any touching. Fresh pasta will only take about 2–3 minutes to cook.

Add the tomato sauce to a frying pan, adding in a little ladle of pasta cooking water to help it to come to temperature. Add the cooked pasta to the tomato sauce. Add a good glug of olive oil and throw in the basil leaves. Give it all a nice toss to help the tomato sauce cling to the pasta. Plate up and shower with really good Parmesan to serve.

Carbonara

Here's one that everyone gets wrong. We grew up on carbonara sauce out of a little plastic bottle and Mum would just cut in some ham and serve it with garlic bread, like I feel every other British household does. What is our obsession with serving Italian food with store-bought baguettes filled with mystery green butter and forgetting about them in the oven?!

Anyway, this is carbonara done properly. Shout-out to the Romans.

SERVES 2

100g/3½oz guanciale, cubed
2 egg yolks
30g/1oz Parmesan cheese, finely grated
1 teaspoon freshly cracked black pepper, plus extra to serve (optional)
250g/9oz penne
salt

Start off by bringing a pan of salted water up to a rolling boil.

Slowly render the guanciale in a cold pan over a medium heat. The guanciale will become glassy as it renders – we're looking for it to colour on all sides, but we don't want it to go completely crispy. Just give it a nice little golden suntan.

Add the egg yolks, cheese, and a couple cracks of pepper to a bowl. Don't worry about mixing them, just leave them be.

Cook the pasta for a minute less than the packet instructions, keeping the guanciale warm without burning it.

Turn the heat up to high on the guanciale, add in your pasta and a few spoons of pasta cooking water. Toss the pasta and the guanciale together so the pasta water thickens with the fat from the guanciale. Do this over a high heat; I don't add the eggs and cheese to the pan because I feel like it's tempting fate.

Add the pasta and guanciale to the bowl with the eggs and cheese. Add a little spoon of pasta water and stir the whole thing together until smooth and silky. If you feel like your sauce is too wishy-washy, add it to the pan and toss it. The residual heat in your pan will thicken the sauce.

I like to serve my carbonara loose but silky; if the sauce is too thick the pasta will go cold too quickly and start to solidify. I serve mine with another little crack of pepper on top.

Agnolotti with Leftover Ragù

I put this dish on as a special at Palatino once and I've been making it ever since. You can make this with any leftover ragù or even if you have any leftover filling from the raviolis on page 140. Before I got to head chef and had to worry about profit margins, I'd put dried porcini in everything. Then I realized how much they cost and hid them from the team and myself. (I'd put fucking porcini in staff food.) But also, don't get me started on some of the shit staff food chefs make. I made staff food almost every day at Palatino just because I wanted something edible. I'd enjoy Tuesdays and Thursdays the most when Massimo was in, everything Massimo touched was always delicious.

SERVES 4

1 quantity Rich Egg Yolk Pasta
    Dough (see page 120)
330g/11½oz ragù (see page 144)
50g/1¾oz dried porcini
    mushrooms
olive oil
75g/2¾oz butter
30g/1oz flat-leaf parsley, finely
    chopped, plus extra to garnish
juice of ½ lemon
Parmesan cheese, to serve

Agnolotti isn't the easiest pasta shape to make, but I'm going to try to break it down so that it makes sense for you. Start off by rolling out the pasta dough down to level 2 (see page 147) – you want the sheet of pasta to be at least 60cm/24in long.

Put your ragù in a piping bag, cut off the end of the piping bag so it's 2cm/¾in wide. Pipe one solid line of ragù all the way along the pasta dough. Spray the dough with a little water. Fold the edge of the pasta dough over the ragù and make sure it's tucked in around the filling so that the filling is fully encased. Starting from one end, and using both your hands, pinch the dough every 5cm/2in so you've made little encased pillows of filling. Now, where you have pinched, you're going to cut with a zig-zag pasta cutter. As you cut, the pasta will naturally fold in on itself, making a little mouth-shaped indentation. The pasta that's now on the bottom, leave a couple millimetres overhang so they sit up. Cut that with the same cutter. (I think I've made this sound easy. I'll do a video on Sunday Sessions and, if you get stuck, refer to that.)

Repeat until you have about 20 agnolotti.

For the sauce, rehydrate the porcini in 150ml/5fl oz boiling water for about 5 minutes until they're soft. Separate the rehydrated mushrooms from the stock, strain the stock and save it for the sauce.

Bring a pan of salted water to the boil for the pasta and, once boiling, add the agnolotti.

In a frying pan, heat a little olive oil until it's almost smoking. Add the soaked porcini and fry until they have caramelized and picked up a little colour. Add the butter and let it melt, then add half the mushroom stock. Turn up the heat so that the liquid starts to thicken. Add your cooked agnolotti and swirl them about in the stock. If your liquid is too loose, crank up the heat and keep swirling the pan around. Once the liquid is starting to thicken, add the parsley and lemon juice. Plate up, garnish with a little extra parsley and grate over the Parmesan.

Fennel Sausage Ragù and Cavatelli

This is a southern Italian classic, deep and rich. Listen, in my house we don't cook dishes to feed just the household. The boys will often shout me, 'What you saying? What's cooking?' I always cook more when it comes to ragù. Feed all your people or eat it on toast for breakfast with a fried egg and loads of Parmesan. Or stick it in the freezer.

SERVES 6

200g/7oz diced pancetta
olive oil
5 red onions, finely diced
5 celery sticks, finely diced
4 fennel bulbs, finely diced
5 garlic cloves, thinly sliced
2 tbsp fennel seeds
1 heaped tbsp chilli flakes
1.6kg/3lb 8oz fennel sausages, casings removed
160ml/5¼fl oz red wine
4 x 400g/14oz cans tomatoes, drained
½ quantity Semolina Pasta Dough (see page 120)
750g/1lb 10oz cavatelli
good-quality olive oil, for finishing
a handful of flat-leaf parsley, very finely chopped
salt

I start a lot of my ragùs with diced pancetta – why just cook in olive oil when you can cook everything in pork fat? Add the diced pancetta to a high-sided saucepan over a medium heat with a glug of olive oil. Gently fry off the pancetta until it's fully rendered and super golden and crispy all over. Add the onion, celery and fennel and cook the vegetables over a medium heat for about 1½ hours – I know that sounds like a long time but, if you don't, you won't build any flavour. The veg will cook in stages – when you first add it to the pancetta the frying will die down and the veg will release all of their water. The veg will eventually start to fry again and become translucent. Keep cooking until the mixture is brown and sticky. Taste it – you want it to be sweet before we add everything else. If you don't make a good base for a ragù, you are never going to make something amazing.

When your base is dark and sweet, add the garlic, fennel seeds and chilli flakes. Cook for 5 minutes, making sure you don't get any colour on the garlic. We want the chilli flakes and fennel seeds to fry off in the oil and flavour everything. Next, add your peeled fennel sausages and fry them off. Again, the sausages will cook in stages. When you add them, the pan temperature drops, then the pan slowly starts to come back up to temperature and the sausages release their water. The water evaporates and the sausage start to fry again. You want the sausages to be cooked off before we stew them.

Add the wine and reduce. Add the tomatoes, crank up the heat and bring to the boil, then reduce the heat and simmer for 1½ hours to cook off all the moisture. I always cook the moisture out of my ragùs because we will be adding pasta water later when we finish them.

To make the cavaletti, roll the dough into a long thin sausage about your thumbs' fingernail in diameter. Cut the sausage into 1cm/⅓in pieces. Now, you can order a pasta paddle online for a few quid or roll the pasta down the back of a fork. Coat the little piece of dough in semolina and, whichever way you're doing it, roll the little piece of dough down the grooves. The semolina pasta will be good for up to three days in the fridge and you're better off making more than not enough.

Bring a large saucepan of heavily salted water up to the boil. Heat two big kitchen spoons of your ragù in a frying pan. Drop your pasta into the water. As it's fresh, it will only need to boil for about 4 minutes. Once your ragu is warm, loosen it with pasta water before adding the cooked cavatelli. Toss the pasta and the ragù together; you want it to be wet and it needs to sound sexy as you toss it together. Finish the ragu with a good glug of olive oil and chopped parsley.

Amatriciana

I love pastas that are made from about four ingredients. Pasta is about simplicity, sourcing the best ingredients and cooking them correctly. Pork, garlic, fresh tomatoes and Pecorino. You don't really need much else. If you can't get guanciale, honestly don't bother bro. This dish is all about celebrating its fatty, salty, peppery flavour as the guanciale bleeds into the tomato sauce. Also, any leftover sauce, stick it on top of some toasted sourdough. Shit BANGS!

SERVES 4

1.4kg/3lb 3oz San Marzano
   tomatoes
200g/7oz guanciale
55g/2oz garlic cloves, thinly
   sliced
1 tsp chilli flakes
10 fresh basil leaves
500g/1lb 2oz fresh spaghetti
good-quality olive oil, for
   finishing
Pecorino cheese

Start off by coring the tomatoes and making a little X on their bums with a knife. We are going to blanch the tomatoes to get the skin off.

Bring a pan of water to the boil and drop the tomatoes in. Your water has to be boiling. Don't put all the tomatoes in all at once as the water temperature will drop and they'll basically sit in a warm bath. Drop the tomatoes in, four at a time and boil them for 2 minutes.

Once the tomatoes are boiled, lift them out of the water and plunge them straight into iced water to stop the cooking process and help shrink the skin. Peel the tomatoes under the iced water. You'll feel the skin come off and the flesh underneath will be floury, rub that stuff off as it makes the sauce a little weird in the mouth. Take the tomatoes out of the water and squash them into a bowl, just to break them apart.

Take the skin off the guanciale and cut it into quite chunky cubes, like sugar cubes. Stick a frying pan over a medium heat and add the guanciale. Don't worry about the pan heating up. We want to render the fat out of our guanciale to cook the remaining bits. The guanciale will bleed out and start to look see through. Crisp it up a little on all the sides; I don't go super crispy on the guanciale, I like the chew of it when the sauce is finished. Add the garlic and the chilli flakes. Let them fry gently without colouring – we want the flavour of the garlic to carry in the pork fat. The garlic will let out all its sugar and when you stir the mix it will start to clump. Add your squashed tomatoes, crank up the heat and bring it to the boil. Once the mixture is boiling, drop the heat to a low–medium and let it bubble away gently. We simmer the sauce until the all the moisture from the tomatoes is cooked off and you're left with a thick, deep red sauce. Stir through the basil.

Bring a large saucepan of water up to the boil, the pasta needs room so that each piece can cook uniformly. Make sure your pasta water is heavily salted. We've put all that effort into making a delicious sauce, we need to make sure the pasta is singing too. Heat the sauce in a frying pan and add a couple ladles of the pasta water. Once the sauce has come up to heat, turn it down just to keep it warm. Boil the spaghetti until it's al dente, then add to the sauce with another ladle of pasta water. Crank the heat up to high and toss the pasta and the sauce together. You're not folding the two ingredients together but more agitating them to get the sauce to thicken. That first ladle of pasta water will get completely sucked up by the pasta continuing to cook in the pan. Add another little glug of pasta water and stir until the mix is glossy. I finish all my pasta' with a generous glug of olive oil. IF YOUR PASTA LOOKS DRY IN THE PAN IT WILL BE DRY ON THE PLATE. Your pasta should be nice and loose before it hits the plate, otherwise it will just seize up. Grate over the Pecorino. Finito.

Lobster Ravioli and Bisque

So here's something a little bouji; I don't actually expect any of you to make this as it pretty much takes all bloody day. However, if you do decide to, then invite someone over who you love, someone who means something to you, someone that you'd ride or die for. I ate this with Little Hus in the garden with a couple of glasses of white wine, talking future, laughing about the past and enjoying the moment. BIG UP Huseyin – that's bloodline!

SERVES 2

½ quantity Rich Egg Yolk Pasta
    Dough (see page 120)
semolina, for dusting
peppery olive oil, for drizzling
salt

For the filling
1kg/2lb 4oz lobster
a good pinch of sea salt
zest of 1 lemon
5g/⅛oz chopped flat-leaf parsley
300g/10½oz prawns, blitzed
1 egg white

For the bisque
1 lobster shell
1 crab shell
olive oil, for frying
2 fennel bulbs, chopped
3 white onions, chopped
4 celery sticks, chopped
3 carrots, peeled and chopped
5 garlic cloves, peeled and
    chopped
12g/½oz fresh thyme
2 fresh bay leaves
100ml/3½fl oz Hennessy cognac
200ml/7fl oz white wine
1 tbsp tomato purée
240g/8½oz tomatoes, freshly
    grated
6 litres/10½ pints Chicken
    Stock (see page 16) or fish
    stock or water
2 tbsp crème fraîche

To garnish
16 pieces of samphire
½ fennel bulb, finely sliced on a
    mandoline
juice of ½ lemon

If you make either of the crab
recipes (see pages 24 and 124)
please save the crab shells and
freeze them for this.

You have to make this recipe with a
live lobster, so you're going to have
to kill it. There's a little line that
runs along the top of the lobster's
head. Stick the knife in the crease
closest to the tail end. Plunge the
knife straight through the lobster's
head and then cut down so the
head is cut in half. Hold the claws,
then give them a twist and they'll
come right off. Leave the tail
attached to the head – we don't
want to expose the flesh and dilute
the flavour into the water.

Bring a large pan of water to the boil
and season the water so it tastes
like the sea. Make sure the water is
at a rolling boil. Drop in the lobster's
body, stick a lid on and boil it hard
for 4 minutes.

Once the lobster has boiled, it
needs to go straight into ice to stop
the cooking process – this also
makes getting the meat out of the
shell a lot easier.

Break the claws down raw; you're
gonna need something heavy and a
pair of scissors. Break open the
claws and cut open all the knuckles.
Scoop out the raw meat with a
spoon and give it a quick whizz in a
blender. We are going to use this to
bind our mix together.

To get the tail meat out of the
cooked lobster, hold the head still
with your left hand and twist the
body with your right hand and pull
away. Run a pair of sharp scissors
down the tail, cutting the shell down
the middle on both sides. Pull the
cut sides apart and there you go –
one cooked lobster tail. If there's
any stuff in your lobster tail, just run
it under the tap – it doesn't matter if

it's green or orange, just rinse it
off. Chop the lobster tail into
small pieces; I just run a knife
over mine until it's the same size
as mincemeat.

Add your raw claw meat to the
cooked cold lobster and place in a
blender with the salt, lemon zest and
parsley. Add the prawns and blitz
until smooth. Then add the egg white
and mix through thoroughly. You
don't want to blitz it for long, just
until it's incorporated. Stick the mix
in a piping bag and chill in the fridge.

Preheat the oven to 180°C
fan/200°C/ 400°F/gas mark 6.

Rinse the lobster's head under the
tap and take out everything, leaving
just the shell.

To make the bisque, roast the
lobster and crab shells in the oven
for 20 minutes until they've dried
out and the smell of roasting shells
perfumes the kitchen. DO NOT burn
the shells.

While the shells are roasting,
roughly cut up all your veg and the
garlic – it's only for a stock, no
beauty points here.

Heat a little olive oil in a heavy-
based high-sided saucepan. Add all
your veg and fry over a medium heat
for about 20 minutes – we want
good colour on the base. Add the
thyme and bay once you've got a
golden colour on the veg. Then stick
the roasted shells into the mix. Add
the Hennessy and, using a long
match, light the alcohol – you want
to light the Hennessy as soon as it
goes in the pan; if you add it and
then scurry around the kitchen

looking for a flame, you'll make yourself a fireball and end up with no eyebrows, lashes or worse. Once the flame is fully burnt off, add your white wine and allow the liquid to reduce. Add the tomato purée and give the base a good stir. Fry for 2 minutes, stirring it through to coat the veg. Add the grated tomato next and fry for another 2 minutes. Cover the base with enough of the chicken or fish stock or water just to cover the bones and bring to the boil. Once boiling, drop the heat to medium and allow to cook for at least 2 hours. We want it to cook slow to extract all the flavour we have put in the pan.

After 2 hours, the liquid should have reduced by half. Strain out all the bones and veg through a sieve. Strain the stock again through a clean cloth or muslin – we don't want any bits at all, we just want clean liquid. Reduce the stock over a high heat until it starts to thicken. Don't turn your back on the stock in the later stages as the last thing you want to do is over-reduce the liquid and end up with a teaspoon of bisque. The more the stock reduces down, the more the taste and colour intensifies. I reduce mine until it becomes viscous, syrupy and a deep mahogany colour. Taste it at this point – it should be deep, mouth-coating, sticky and on the verge of being overpowering. I don't season my bisque as we are going to season the pasta water and we have already seasoned our raviolo filling. Finish the bisque with the crème fraîche – it will change the colour and give the bisque that bit of sharp acidity that it needs for it not to be too punchy. Look at you, you've made a classic French sauce. Long ting but easy right?

Roll out the pasta dough to the number 2 setting, working your way down the settings on the machine. Cut the length of pasta you have in half.

The crab filling will make 2 big raviolos. Using a large mug as a stencil, pipe the filling on to the pasta in a circular motion. Spray the pasta with water so that you have an even spread of water. Lay the second sheet of pasta over the top of the filling. I work left to right when working with pasta. I cup my hand in a cup shape. Working on the left side of the ravioli, I'll press the C shape around half the pasta and then press it down with my fingertips so I know that one side is secure. I gently pull the remaining pasta so that I can cup the air out of the side that is open. We don't want any air in our pasta as this can cause it to burst. Cup your hand around the other side of the pasta, nudging the filling into the middle. Once you've secured the other side, press your finger all the way around it to make sure it's fully secured. Using the mug as a stencil again, cut the raviolos out with it.

Bringing a large pan of salted water up to a rolling boil, then add the pasta and cook for 4½ minutes. Add the samphire for the last 15 seconds of cooking. Pull the pasta and samphire out of the pan and rest them on a clean tea towel to dry slightly. Put the pasta on the plates first, then pour a good couple tablespoons of bisque over the top and add a few bits of samphire. Dress the shaved fennel in the lemon juice and stick that on top for height. I then drizzle a little bit of peppery olive oil over the top. Enjoy! TENKS.

Ragù and Pappardelle

Listen, I've worked with more Italians than the fucking embassy. Everyone does it different, everyone else's is wrong, blah blah blah. We all need to know how to make a proper ragù. I say proper, but let's say decent, coz someone somewhere is turning in their grave saying, 'He's doing it wrong'. Honestly, I'm absolutely sick of making them, BUT it's something we should all have in our repertoires as, from 'spag bol' to lasagne, a good ragù is a game-changer. If I had an Italian nonna, I'm sure I'd get a little cheeky smile and a wink for the skills. Love you imaginary nonna, this one's for you. *Forza Italia.*

SERVES 4

olive oil
500g/1lb 2oz diced pork shoulder
500g/1lb 2oz diced chuck steak
2 red onions, finely diced
1 white onion, finely diced
2 carrots, finely diced
2 celery sticks, finely diced
4 garlic cloves, thinly sliced
3 g fresh thyme
3 bay leaves
175ml/6fl oz red wine
700g/1lb 9 oz canned tomatoes
1 quantity Rich Egg Yolk Pasta
    Dough (see page 119) or
    400g/14oz dried pappardelle
semolina, for dusting
a handful of flat-leaf parsley, very
    finely chopped
sea salt and black pepper

Start off by seasoning your diced meat heavily with salt and pepper. Stick a high-sided saucepan over a medium heat with a glug of olive oil and seal the meat so it's brown on all sides – no colour = no flavour. Once all the meat is coloured, set to one side and throw in the onions, carrots and celery and fry them off gently. We want a deep colour – we're talking about 45 minutes to build a depth of flavour and sweetness that's gonna run all the way through the ragù. We can't rush this shit. If you make this and it's not nice, it's because you've not cooked the base long enough.

Once the vegetables are dark and sweet but not burnt, add your garlic, thyme and bay leaves and fry for 5 minutes. Add your sealed meat back in, then deglaze the pan with the red wine over a high heat and reduce by half. Add the tomatoes and 600 ml/1 pint water. Bring to the boil and cook over a medium heat for 15 minutes, until the sauce has reduced by half. Add 400ml/14fl oz water, cover with a lid and simmer for at least 2½ hours, until the meat is completely soft and can be pulled apart with a spoon.

Pappardelle is probably the easiest pasta to roll. If you're using pasta dough, roll the dough down to level 2, working your way down number by number and making sure you go through each number twice. Cut the pasta into more manageable lengths – about 30cm/12in. I like pappardelle to be about a finger-width wide, but

you can go for two fingers wide or even a little less – there aren't any rules. Cut the pasta into strips vertically – 125g/4½oz is more than enough per person. Make sure to give the pasta a dusting of semolina once it's done to stop it from all sticking together. You can store the pasta in the fridge for 2 days tops, but I find it's best eaten on the day the dough is made.

If you're using fresh pasta, it'll cook pretty quickly. If you're using dried, go a little fancier and try a dried egg pasta, it's worth the extra couple of quid.

Two tablespoons of ragù is enough for one portion with this one, if you finish a pasta correctly, there doesn't have to be loads of meat in your ragù. Add eight tablepoons of ragù to a frying pan with a couple splashes of your pasta cooking water to loosen it.

Bring a pan of salted water up to a rolling boil. Drop your pasta into the boiling water. Once your pasta is 90% cooked, add it to the ragù. Add another couple of splashes of pasta cooking water as the pasta will suck up all the moisture in the pan. Gently toss the pasta and the ragù together. Once again, the pasta will start to suck up the ragù. Add a little more pasta water and a good few glugs of olive oil. Give it a toss and, when the liquid in the pan starts to thicken, add the parsley. Stir it through and you're good to go.

Ricotta and Lemon Ravioli with Sage Butter

My first day at Palatino, Richard Blackwell stuck me on the pasta section and showed me the pasta bench downstairs. I rolled ravioli until service in a lifeless basement in front of clean white plastic walls, sweat dripping from my brow, managing to get semolina everywhere. 'You're a messy pup aren't you? Where you going Has?' 'I'm running Argos quick, I cant work down there in silence man.' Back from Argos, I plugged my speaker in and got shit popping. I grew a lot at Palatino. As a chef, as a manager, and, most importantly, as a person. Rich, who was a senior chef at Fifteen, he knew how us graduates get on. Yeah, we come with baggage, sometimes we're hard to deal with, but we always make it happen. Rich would just let me get on with things, he trusted me, and knew bollocking me wouldn't get us anywhere. I love Rich for everything he did for me, for teaching me the super boring side of running a restaurant, but also for just letting me listen to heavy grime at 8 a.m., and knowing I'd have 50 portions done by staff breakfast. Anyway, I'm waffling, but basically thank you Richard Blackwell for letting me buy a speaker x

SERVES 4

½ quantity Rich Egg Yolk Pasta
  Dough (see page 120)
semolina, for dusting (optional)
100g/3½oz butter
8 sage leaves

For the filling
300g/10½oz ricotta
30g/1oz Parmesan cheese, grated,
  plus extra to serve
zest of 1 lemon
a good crack of sea salt and black
  pepper

For the filling, mix all the ingredients together in a bowl. I like to use sheep's ricotta for that extra acidic twang. Stick the mix in a piping bag and set aside in the fridge.

Listen, rolling pasta is pretty easy. Anyone can do it, but there's a few rules:

1. Try to work on a wooden bench or a heavily semolina-coated work surface.

2. Don't just put the pasta dough through the machine once and work all the way down. Always go through each number at least twice. We want to laminate or fold our dough to build the gluten and give us a good chew.

3. Making pasta in the summer is pretty shit – try to either do it early in the morning or late in the evening, ready for the next day.

4. Relax fam, don't start stressing out. Pasta is a labour of love. Stick on some tunes and take your time. You're not cooking for the rassclart queen or Hus, in my case. Hus is super critical but can't even make a sandwich.

5. Always rest the pasta on the back of your hand when working with it, you want to treat it with the highest respect. We don't want fingerprints or to stretch the dough while moving it, otherwise you'll have inconsistent spots that will just bite you on the arse later.

OK, so now we've got that out of the way, let's talk about rolling your pasta out, getting the filling in and shaping properly.

I like to start off by running my pasta through the machine from level 10 to about level 7, running the pasta through twice each time. You'll see that your ends are a weird shape and pasta is a lot easier to work with in straight lines. Working from left to right, fold your pasta back on itself, like you're folding a tea towel. Take the setting back up to 10, semolina your bench and work through each number twice, making sure to semolina every now and then. Yeah, it gets messy, but do you want nice pasta or not?

Take the pasta all the way down to level 2. If the sheet is too long for your work space, you can fold the pasta – just let it fall naturally on itself, making sure there's semolina on any bits of pasta that are touching.

Pipe little 25g/1oz balls of filling just above the centre along the pasta sheet, leaving a 4-finger gap in-between each one.

Using a spray bottle filled with water, give the pasta a good spray to help it stick together. Lift the bottom edge of the pasta and fold it upwards, again letting the pasta fall naturally. You don't want any heavy hands at this point. You'll see that some of the pasta is creased. Go along and straighten the pasta so that it's all level. Working from left to right, push the left-hand side of the pasta down to trap the filling, with your other hand giving the sheet of pasta a little tug to release any air. The idea is that you are securing the pasta without retaining any air in the filling. Work around each piece slowly. If you find that the pasta is creased over the filling, you can give it a gentle pull from the top. Seal all the filling down first. Then push down the remaining pasta. Cut the pasta into squares with a fluted pasta cutter, trimming a little off the top. I don't like mine super compact, like ravioli from a tin. We've spent all that time making dough, rolling and filling, so we want to taste the pasta.

Bring a pan of heavily salted water up to a rolling boil and cook the ravioli for 2 minutes until they float. Melt the butter in a large frying pan until it slowly starts to foam, then add the sage leaves. When the sage perfumes the air and starts to soften with no colour, add in a ladleful of pasta cooking water. Crank up the heat so that the buttery water emulsifies. Add the cooked ravioli and swirl them about until the butter thickens.

Serve four ravioli per person and a couple sage leaves each. Grate over some more Parmesan. Classic. You're welcome.

Pork Shoulder and 'Nduja Ragù

This dish is inspired by a meal once made by Chris Leechy, head chef at Manteca. I'd never had 'nduja in a ragù, nor had I ever seen garganelli. It just all made sense. I guessed the process and now we're here.

SERVES 6

1.5kg/3lb 5oz pork shoulder, cut into 2.5cm/1in dice
olive oil, for frying
5 carrots, finely diced
4 white onions, finely diced
½ head of celery, finely diced
14 garlic cloves, thinly sliced
5g/⅛oz thyme leaves
10g/¼oz chopped rosemary
4 bay leaves
300g/10½oz 'nduja
250ml/9fl oz white wine
3 x 400g/14oz cans whole tomatoes, drained
sea salt and black pepper

To serve

6 portions of cooked pasta (I like garganelli)
sourdough breadcrumbs
zest of ½ lemon

Start off by seasoning and sealing your diced pork in olive oil in a high-sided pan. Make sure your oil is hot before you go in with the meat. Don't put all the meat in at once – cook it in little batches to keep the oil hot and crisp up the pork, then set aside the cooked pork.

Once all the pork is sealed, add the diced carrot, onion, and celery to the pan. Lower the heat to medium, add a big pinch of salt and cook for 35–40 minutes. We want our base to be deep and delicious but not burnt. Slow cooking is going to bring out the sweetness in the veg. Once the base vegetables are cooked, add the garlic, thyme, rosemary and bay leaves. Gently fry for 5 minutes – you don't want any colour on the garlic; garlic goes from releasing its sugar and being super sweet to bitter very quickly, so be diligent.

Add your sealed pork back to the pan and stir it through the cooked veg. Break in the 'nduja and allow it to melt – the cooking oil will turn a beautiful red. Keep stirring and let the pork warm up again. Give the mixture a taste – it should be sweet, spicy and meaty. Turn the heat up so you're frying hard again without letting the base catch, then add your white wine. Let the white wine boil and reduce completely. Do not stop stirring; do not let anything catch. Add your drained tomatoes, then fill the three cans with water and add that too. Bring the ragù to the boil, then turn the heat to low and let the ragù slowly blip away. Cook the ragù for 2 hours, or until the pork fully pulls apart with no resistance. We want to cook all the moisture out of the ragù so that the flavour intensifies.

I serve my ragù with garganelli, sourdough breadcrumbs and a couple strikes of lemon zest.

Rotolo

This is one that we used to do at Palatino on the set Christmas menu. I was the rotolo man. I just enjoyed rolling up pasta until service, with the tunes on in the basement, making an incredible mess. This is defo one to do if you've got people coming over. It's a lot more manageable than trying to cook everyone pasta at the same time. Roll it, poach it, slice it. Look like the dog's bollocks.

SERVES 10

700g/1lb 9oz butternut squash, peeled and cut into 5cm/2in cubes
100g/3½oz cherry tomatoes
10g/¼oz sea salt
9g/¼oz sage
50ml/2fl oz olive oil
3 garlic cloves, smashed
1 tsp chilli flakes
1 quantity Rich Egg Yolk Pasta Dough (see page 120)
semolina, for dusting
Parmesan cheese, grated, to serve

For the filling
600g/1lb 5oz spinach
500g/1lb 2oz ricotta
10g/¼oz sea salt
2 pinches of pepper
½ tsp grated nutmeg
30g/1oz Parmesan cheese, grated

To garnish
olive oil
100g/3½oz chanterelle mushrooms, whole
1 garlic clove, sliced
150g/5½oz butter
10 sage leaves

Preheat the oven to 160°C fan/180°C/350°F/gas mark 4.

Put the squash in a bowl and add the tomato, salt, sage, olive oil, garlic and chilli flakes. Give it all a good mix, transfer to a roasting tray and roast for 35 minutes until completely soft. Once cooked, smash it all together and allow to cool.

For the spinach filling, blanch the spinach in heavily salted water, then drain and shock it in iced water. Once cold, squeeze out all the moisture and give it a good chop. Transfer this to a bowl, add the ricotta, salt, pepper, nutmeg and Parmesan and mix together.

Roll the pasta dough all the way down to level 3 on your pasta machine, making sure that you've done every number twice. We need to make 2 lengths of pasta that are the same width as a tea towel. Lay out a clean tea towel and dust it with semolina so the pasta doesn't stick after cooking. Put the first sheet of pasta 5cm/2in above the bottom of your tea towel. Put the bottom of the second sheet on top of the previous sheet, overlapping them by about 1cm/½in and using water to seal them so you've now got one big rectangle of pasta dough. Don't bother pushing it down or anything – it will hold. Spread the spinach filling evenly across the first pasta sheet and do the same with the squash on the second sheet. Roll the entire thing as if you were rolling a spliff, a roll

of baking paper or a jam roly-poly. You should be left with a big pasta sausage. Bring the sausage down to the base of the tea towel. Roll the tea towel the same way you did the pasta and, using butcher's string and starting from one end of the rotolo, tie it off nice and tight. Do this all the way down the length about eight times. The middle knots shouldn't be super tight, otherwise the pasta will split; the ones on each end are to keep the water out.

Bring a big pan of salted water up to the boil, then drop in the rotolo (in the tea towel) and simmer for 12 minutes. Traditionally, you'd use a rotolo pan but I use a large saucepan. Turn off the heat and leave the rotolo in the water while we work on the garnish.

In a super-hot frying pan, add a little glug of olive oil and your chanterelles. Fry the mushrooms hard for a good 4 minutes, rolling them around the pan. Once the mushrooms have started to brown a little, season with salt, add the garlic and fry for a couple seconds, then add the butter and sage leaves. Bring the butter up to foaming point, then reduce the heat and let the butter slowly brown.

Pull the rotolo out of the water. Cut off the string, unroll the tea towel and portion the rotolo into slices two fingers' wide. Lay them face-down on warm plates, spoon over a few mushrooms and the brown butter and finish with grated Parmesan.

SOMETHING TO FINISH

Grandma's Parkin

SERVES 14

225g/8oz unsalted butter
280g/10oz good-quality
   golden syrup
55g/2oz black treacle
115g/4oz caster sugar
225g/8oz fine oatmeal
225g/8oz plain flour
2 level tsp baking powder
2 heaped tsp ground ginger
1 large egg
a glug of full-fat milk, to
   loosen (optional)

Most of these recipes have been about the Cypriot side of my family – beautiful holidays and family memories. However, a lot of good food came from my mum and grandma. We would go to Grandma's almost every Sunday as kids (before Dad got sick of roasts and decided to BBQ) and Grandma would make traditional roast dinner with all the trimmings, Shepherd's pie, and sometimes these bad boy curried turkey pancakes – sounds weird but they're great.

My earliest food memory is of my grandma in her kitchen in Palmers Green. It was just me and Grandma, which didn't happen often when you're the youngest of three. Grandma was making me a sandwich (also Grandma makes a banging sandwich and taught me to season the bread and butter; proper veteran move) and I was banging on about how she didn't have any crisps. From her fridge she pulled a beetroot, a parsnip and a potato and she made crisps for me, and they were banging. Grandma always went that extra mile when it came to cooking and still does to this day. BIG UP JANET EACH AND EVERY TIME!

Preheat the oven to 130°C fan/150°C/300°F/ gas mark 2.

In a saucepan over a gentle heat, melt the butter, golden syrup, black treacle and sugar together. Once melted, allow to cool a little. Next, place all the dry ingredients in a bowl and add the syrup. Beat 1 large egg and add to the mix. The mix should resemble a batter; if the mix is too tight, add a little splash of milk to loosen.

Line a high-edged baking tray (28 x 23 x 5cm/11 x 8 x 2in) with greaseproof baking paper and pour in the parkin mixture. Bake on the second shelf up from the bottom of the oven for 1 hour 15 minutes or until the parkin is fully brown and set. It will keep well in a sealed container and will improve with keeping. We grew up eating this as is, and Grandma still makes it for every family get-together. It's also great with custard or ice cream, or as a cheeky afternoon snack with a wedge of cheese.

Lemon Meringue Pie

I used to make a good few lemon tarts a week at Palatino and so when the boys asked me to make one at home, I decided to do a lemon meringue pie so that it didn't feel like I was at work. It went down a treat. So here you have it – LMP, ladies and gents.

SERVES 12

For the pastry
350g/12oz plain flour
250g/9oz unsalted butter
100g/3½oz icing sugar
3 egg yolks
1 egg, beaten

For the lemon curd
zest and juice of 7½ lemons
225g/8oz cold unsalted
 butter, cubed
6 egg yolks
4 eggs
250g/9oz caster sugar

For the meringue
225g/8oz egg whites
450g/1lb sugar

Start with the pastry. In a mixer, add your plain flour and butter and mix until it starts to resemble breadcrumbs. Go in with the icing sugar next. Add your egg yolks one by one until the dough comes together. Once the dough has come together, turn the mixer off – you don't want to overwork the pastry. Roll the dough into a sausage, wrap in clingfilm and allow to freeze solid.

Once the dough is frozen, grate it into a 30cm/12in tart tin. Start off by pushing the dough into the edges of the tart tin – I push mine into the grooves, working from the bottom up. Keep pushing the pastry into the gaps until the tart tin is completely covered. Poke loads of holes in the base with a fork to stop the pastry from rising but don't worry about levelling off the dough around the rim as we will trim that once the tart is baked. Chill the tart briefly in the fridge.

Preheat the oven to 140°C fan/160°C/325°F/gas mark 3.

Once chilled, line the pastry with baking paper and fill with baking beans. Cook the tart case for 25–30 minutes. Once the rim starts to colour, take out the baking beans. Egg wash the tart with the beaten egg and bake for a further 20 minutes. We want our tart case to be fully cooked through as it won't be going back in the oven. Once it's completely brown, allow the tart to cool and move on to the lemon curd.

Place the lemon zest and juice in a pan and reduce by half – do this gently so it turns darker and syrupy. Once reduced, slowly add in cubes of cold butter one by one, whisking them in until the mixture thickens.

In a separate bowl, mix the yolks and whole eggs together.

Once all the butter is melted into the syrup, add a little bit of the hot syrup to the eggs and whisk. By doing this we are just tempering the eggs so that they don't scramble in the pan. Now tip the egg mix into the syrup over a low heat. With a plastic spatula, keep the mixture moving, making sure you scrape the bottom of the pan so that nothing sticks. Keep slowly cooking the curd for 5–8 minutes – it is ready when you can run your spatula along the base and it leaves a trail and the mix slowly comes back together. Take off the heat and keep the curd moving. Pour the curd into the pastry case and chill in the fridge until fully cooled.

For the meringue, make sure the bowl of your food mixer is clean and dry. Using the whisk attachment, whip the egg whites on medium speed for about 5 minutes until they're fluffy. Meanwhile, add the sugar and 150ml (5fl oz) water to a pan. Bring the sugar and water to the boil and, using a sugar thermometer, take your syrup up to 120°C/248°F. Allow the syrup to stand for a couple minutes, then slowly drizzle it down the side of the bowl while whipping on a high speed. Once all the syrup has been added, beat the meringue until the mixture is completely cool. This takes a while. We need to keep whipping until you can touch the bowl of the mixer without it burning you. The meringue needs to be fluffy and elastic.

Now it's up to you – you can pipe the meringue on to the pie or you can just do what I do and slap it in the middle and spread it out. Then the fun bit is using a cook's blowtorch to torch the meringue until you get beautiful cooked marshmallow colours. Let the pie sit for a bit before cutting it. Just enough time for you to admire it in all its beauty.

Lokma

As you can probably tell, I'm hardly a pastry wizard, so I've just stuck a few baking recipes in the book that I like eating and that I would also consider pretty easy. Foolproof, if you will. I think the only way to describe lokma is 'doughnut-ish things dipped in syrup' (insert shrugging emoji). Turks are renowned for making sweet things sweeter just by dunking them in syrup. We would eat lokma hot out of the frying pan on summer evenings when we'd all be at my nan's. Mine are nowhere near as good as hers, but I gave it my best shot.

SERVES 6

600g/1lb 5oz plain flour
1 tbsp caster sugar
1 tbsp cornflour
7g packet of dried fast-action
   yeast
1.5 litres/2¾ pints vegetable oil
a pinch of sea salt

For the syrup
600g/1lb 5oz caster sugar
juice of ½ lemon

Mix the flour, sugar and cornflour in a big mixing bowl and make a well in the middle. Add the dried yeast to the well, pour in 600ml/1 pint tepid water and whisk until completely smooth. It will be quite runny, but basically you want it to be a thick batter consistency. Cover the batter in clingfilm and let it prove for at least 2 hours at room temperature.

For the syrup, add the sugar with 140ml/19fl oz water to a saucepan and bring to the boil. Once boiling, allow to boil for at least 15 minutes, then add the lemon juice.

To cook, heat the vegetable oil to 180–190°C/350–375°F. We need the oil to be hot so the lokma can cook quickly and the yeast becomes light and fluffy. Pick up the flour mix in your hand and squeeze it until the batter pokes out of the little hole between your index finger and thumb (like your hand is a piping bag). Using a wet teaspoon, scoop ½ teaspoon of batter into the hot oil. Do about eight at a time and cook for 4–5 minutes until they are golden and crispy. Allow the dough balls to drain off, then quickly dunk them straight in the syrup, pull them out and stack them in a bowl.

These are best eaten hot, crispy and dripping with syrup.

Ricotta and Semolina Cake

This is the only cake I've ever baked in my life. It was a cake that was run as a special at Palatino and every time I made it, it sank. I did it at home and, instead of baking it in a cake tin, I did it in a tray and it worked. So here. Here's a cake recipe. I hope it doesn't sink.

SERVES 10

400g/14oz caster sugar
350g/12oz unsalted butter
200g/7oz ricotta
6 eggs
zest and juice of 2 lemons
600g/1lb 5oz ground almonds
1 teaspoon baking powder

Preheat the oven to 180°C fan/200°C/350°F/gas mark 4.

Place the sugar and butter in the bowl of a food mixer with a whisk attachment and cream togther – you want the butter to be fluffy but smooth.

In a separate bowl, fold together the ricotta, eggs, lemon juice and lemon zest. It's gonna look like it's split, but it's fine – trust me.

With the mixer still mixing the sugar and butter, slowly add in the ricotta and egg mix little by little, then turn off the mixer. Add the ground almonds and baking powder but do this by hand as we want to keep the cake batter nice and airy. If you do this in the mixer, you'll knock out all the air and the cake will sink.

Line a high-edged baking tray (28 x 23 x 5cm/11 x 8 x 2in) with greaseproof paper, then pour in the cake batter and spread it out so that the top is nice and level. Bake in the oven for 1 hour and 10 minutes.

Let the cake rest once it's cooked. It's quite a moist cake so it will look underdone when you cut into it, but it's delicious. Promise.

Sutlac

I've eaten so much sutlac in my life, not often homemade or by any of the aunties. It's usually given to me for free by the kebab-shop guys for being a loyal customer/Turkish. You have to go to kebab shops with your Turkish friends, but if you don't have one, then make one – it'll come in handy for the hook-ups.

SERVES 4

200g/7oz baldo rice
800ml/1⅓ pints full-fat milk (if you can get the good stuff, use the good stuff)
80g/2¾oz caster sugar
1 vanilla pod, scraped
ground cinnamon, for sprinkling

Place the rice in a saucepan and add 500ml/18fl oz cold water. Slowly bring to the boil, stirring the rice to knock the starch out. Normally, you'd soak the rice and rinse it, blah blah blah, but for this we want to keep the starch as we are going to use it to make the rice thick. Boil off the water, stirring it like a risotto. Once you're left with what looks like the beginnings of a risotto, add the first 400ml/14fl oz of milk and gently simmer the rice. Again, stirring to keep it thick. Once the milk has reduced, add in the remaining 400ml/14fl oz milk, the sugar and vanilla pod. Bring the milk to the boil and then take it off the heat.

Using a slotted spoon, fill four clay or ovenproof pots halfway up – we need to leave space to fill with our milky liquid. Pour the remaining liquid into the clay pots, then place in a baking tray with 2.5cm/1in of water and put the grill on full blast. The water is just to make sure that we are cooking the top and the rice doesn't continue cooking. Grill the rice puddings for about 10 minutes, turning every couple minutes until the top forms a skin and starts to caramelize. Set the rice puddings in the fridge until fully cold. Before serving, scatter a little cinnamon over the top. Buff.

Künefe Adana

I feel like my entire life has been one big kebab. Scouting new manual joints, cooking over coals almost every Sunday or being invited to BBQs and handed the tongs. I wanted to treat it a little differently with this recipe, so here I'm making a dessert. Charcoal is great for big chunks of meat slowly rendering and building smoky flavours, however there's room for smoke in desserts too.

Throughout the world, charcoal and open fires aren't just used for cooking meat over metal. In Turkey, we heat up coffee in charcoal-hot sand, in Sri Lanka every household has an outdoor area for cooking over coconut shells in clay pots, in the Far East fires roar under smoking woks adding extra flavours to the 'wok's breath'. Logs, charcoal, and anything else you can get a fire started with are just a heat source. Once the fire's lit, it's up to you what you do with it.

This dish is inspired by *künefe*, a Middle Eastern dessert of shredded wheat, white cheese and pistachio, traditionally cooked in a little metal plate sat on two skewers in a mangal. At this point you're probably a little confused – I know I said dessert and then mentioned cheese but stay with me. *Künefe* is pressed into a disc shape and slowly cooked in butter to crisp the shredded wheat. It's then drowned in a pretty basic syrup, the cheese in the middle isn't like a Cheddar – imagine melty ricotta – it's there for sourness to cut against all the sugar. I could have just cooked it in a really beautiful traditional metal plate over coals, but I wanted to see if I could make it stick to a skewer. So now you're reading this, I guess it's mission accomplished. (This did not happen first time.)

SERVES 2

80g/3oz kadayif (shredded wheat)
150g/5½oz butter, melted
60g/2oz white cheese (beyaz peynir if you've got a local Turkish supermarket or feta), crumbled
30 crushed pistachios
sea salt
ice cream or clotted cream, to serve

For the sour cherries
85g/3oz cherries
zest of 1 lemon, plus juice of ½
2 tbsp sugar syrup (see below)

For the syrup
160g/5¾oz caster sugar
160g/5¾oz honey

You'll notice that the kadayif comes in quite long lengths; I cut the lengths in half as I find them easier to work with.

Try to work with about 20g/¾oz kadayif at a time to make your life easier. Lay your first 20g/¾oz batch on a work surface and spread it out a little to make a rectangle approx. 40 x 12cm/16 x 4½in. Brush with melted butter, making sure the wheat is flat, and then repeat to make a second layer. Your first two layers are only really there to hold your filling. Add the crumbled white cheese and pistachio in a straight line along the middle, leaving about 2.5cm/1in clear on either end. Season with a little bit of sea salt to bring out the sweet and savoury vibe.

Place the top of a flat adana (wide iron) skewer on the bottom right-hand corner of the kadayif and roll on an angle as if you were trying to recreate that barbershop stripe. Keep the kadayif taut as you roll it – you should end up with something that looks like a kofta. Don't worry if there's a bit of cheese or some pistachios exposed – we are gonna continue to wrap with the remaining 40g/1½oz kadayif. Wrap the remaining kadayif around the kofte, covering any exposed parts and making sure you pull it tight. If you don't pull it tight, it will all fall off your skewer. Now any new bits of kadayif

you have added need to be brushed with butter. Keep repeating this process until you run out of butter and kadayif. Chill in the fridge overnight.

To make the sugar syrup, place the sugar and honey with 160ml/5½fl oz water in a saucepan over a low heat and allow to come to the boil. If you do this over a high heat in the beginning, the sugars won't fully dissolve and you'll end up with sugar crystals when you pour it on to your kadayif. Boil the syrup over a low heat for 10 minutes until the water has completely evaporated and the syrup has turned a honey colour.

To make the sour cherries, stone the cherries, discard the stones and then marinate in lemon zest, juice and 2 tablespoons of the hot syrup. Allow to cool and soak up all the flavours.

Light your BBQ – you want a pretty hot fire – a 3 count (see pages 18–19). There's a lot of butter in our kadayif, so we have to be able to control the temperature, otherwise we will have too many butter drips and create a fire. Cook the kadayif as if you were cooking a sis – so no grill underneath, just constantly turning and checking. I grilled mine for about 20 minutes, turning constantly. We don't want to build too much colour in the beginning. The kadayif will slowly start to crisp and turn brown; the butter that doesn't drip off the skewer will cling on to the kadayif and give us a brown butter vibe.

When you're almost at the desired colour, start to slowly warm your syrup. Bringing it to the boil once is enough. Gently slide your kadayif off the skewer into a baking tray and add your syrup. Allow the kadayif to soak up most of the syrup, and don't be scared to spoon it over the top too, but be careful as sugar burns are the worst!

Once the kadayif has sucked up the syrup, cut it in half and stick it on a plate. I serve mine with the sour cherries and mastic ice cream – any ice cream will do – or a little blob of clotted cream. BUFF.

Pistachio Tart

OK, I don't really like desserts. I never get up in the morning and say to myself, 'I really fancy making a cake'. I can only really make tarts to be honest. Working for Stevie Parle, there was always a tart on the menu, and he ran his kitchens River-Café-style. Basically, although you were on, say, the cold starters section in the evening for service, the prep list would be split amongst the team. So I could be making tarts, marinating meat or rolling pasta for someone else's section. Working the same section every day/night is super boring. You become a robot. Saying that, although it kept us entertained, it wasn't great when the person prepping your section was in the shit, which was pretty much every day. Big up all the Stevie Parle dons for this one.

Just off the top, I don't line tarts the way they teach you in college or the way you've seen before. I was taught to make the dough, freeze it and then grate it into the tart case. Honestly, it's the easiest way.

MAKES A 30 CM/12 IN TART/SERVES 9

For the pastry
350g/12oz plain flour
250g/9oz unsalted butter
100g/3½oz icing sugar
3 egg yolks
1 egg, beaten

For the filling
250g/9oz salted butter
200g/7oz crushed pistachios
50g/1¾oz ground almonds
250g/9oz caster sugar
2 eggs
25 cherries, pitted
sea salt

To finish
20g/¾oz honey
140g/5oz Greek yogurt

Start with the pastry. In a mixer, add your plain flour and butter and mix until it starts to resemble breadcrumbs. Go in with the icing sugar next. Add your egg yolks one by one until the dough comes together. Turn the mixer off – you don't want to overwork the pastry. Roll the dough into a sausage, wrap in clingfilm and allow to freeze solid.

Once the dough is frozen, grate it into a 30cm/12in tart tin. Start off by pushing the dough into the edges of the tart tin – I push mine into the grooves, working from the bottom up. Push the pastry into the gaps until the tart tin is completely covered. Poke loads of holes in the base with a fork to stop the pastry from rising but leave the dough around the rim as we will trim that once the tart is baked. Chill briefly in the fridge.

Preheat the oven to 140°C fan/ 160°C/325°F/gas mark 3.

Once chilled, line the pastry with baking paper and fill with baking beans. Cook the tart case for 25–30 minutes. Once the rim starts to colour, take out the baking beans. Egg wash the tart with the beaten egg and bake for a further 20 minutes. Once it's completely brown, allow the tart to cool remove from the tin and move on to the filling. Increase the oven temperature to 170°C fan/190°C/375°F/gas mark 5.

For the filling, it's best to use a mixer with a paddle attachment as we want to get the mix nice and fluffy. Start off by whipping the butter until it's nice and smooth, then add the nuts and

the sugar and beat on a fast speed until the mix is fluffy and pale in colour. Beat your eggs in a separate bowl, then add in three stages. Add one-third of the egg and allow the mixture to beat around the bowl, then stop the mixing and scrape down the sides so everything is being mixed properly. Repeat this process until you're out of egg. The mixture should be light and fluffy. I season my mix with a little crack of salt just so everything sings a little more.

Add your nut mix to your room temperature tart crust, levelling it out. Poke in your cherries and bake for 45 minutes. When you take the tart out, you want it to have a slight wobble in the middle and the edges to be super golden. Leave to cool for 30 minutes in the fridge before cutting.

Serve the tart with the honey and yogurt. Just mix one into the other and job's a good 'un.

* Here's a little side note about this tart – the first time I made it, I was super stoned and turned up at my mate Rob's place with a bag full of 'stolen' cherries that my dad had picked off a neighbour's bush and the rest of the ingredients I had actually paid for. I smashed it out, gave Robert the first slice and he dropped it. Eat this tart on a table and not stood in the garden on a summer's evening smoking spliffs and chatting shit. HAPPY DAYS!

Index

UK/US Glossary

anticlockwise | counterclockwise
aubergine | eggplant

baking beans | dried beans
baking paper | parchment paper
baking tin | baking pan
baking tray | baking sheet
BBQ (v) | grill (to cook on a lit BBQ and
    not under a preheated broiler)
base (of pan) | bottom
black-eyed beans | black-eyed peas
borlotti beans | cranberry beans
French beans | green beans
runner beans | string beans
braising steak | braising beef
beef tomato | beefsteak tomato
beetroot(s) | beet(s)
bicarbonate of soda | baking soda
bin | trash
bite-sized | bite-size

cake mixture | cake batter
cake tin | cake pan
caster sugar | superfine sugar
chicken portions | chicken parts
chilli (pl: chillies) | chile (fresh or dried)
    (pl: chiles)
chilli flakes | chile flakes
chilli oil | chili oil
chilli paste | chili paste
chilli sauce | chili sauce
chips | French fries
chopping board | cutting board
clingfilm | plastic wrap
cooker | stove
cook's knife | chef's knife
coriander (fresh or dried green leaf)
    | cilantro

defrost | thaw

fishmonger's | fish store
flavour | flavor
fridge | refrigerator
fry | cook, sauté or pan-fry (depending
    on recipe)
frying pan | skillet

full-fat milk | whole milk
further | additional (e.g. for an additional
    5 minutes)

goat's cheese | goat cheese
green pepper | green pepper or green
    bell pepper
grilled (adj) | broiled

helim | use provolone
heavy-based | heavy-bottom
hob | stove

iced water | ice water
icing sugar | confectioners' sugar

jam roly poly | steamed jelly roll
joint | large piece of meat with bone;
    roast
jug | pitcher

kebabs | kebabs or kabobs
kitchen cloth | dish towel or kitchen
    towel
kitchen paper | paper towels

measuring jug | measuring cup
mince (beef/lamb) | ground beef/lamb
mould | mold
muslin | cheesecloth

natural yogurt | plain yogurt
nozzle (for a piping bag) | tip

oven ring | burner

packet | package
packet instructions | package
    directions
parcel | pocket or parcel
passata | strained tomatoes (don't
    substitute tomato paste)
pastry | pie dough or pie pastry:
pastry case | pastry shell
Pecorino cheese | Pecorino cheese;
    most often Pecorino Romano
pepper (as in red, green or yellow

pepper) | bell pepper
pestle in a mortar | in a mortar and
    pestle
piping bag | pastry bag
plain flour | all-purpose flour
prawn(s) | shrimp
prove | rise

roughly (chopped) | coarsely (chopped)
roasting tin | roasting pan
rocket | arugula
rubbish | trash

salt beef | corned beef
scum | foam
self-raising flour | self-rising flour
shop | store
shallow-fry | pan-fry
shortcrust pastry | pastry shell
sieve (n.) | strainer or sieve (sifter for
    flour)
single cream | light cream
spatchcock | butterfly
starter | appetizer or starter
spring onions | scallions
stock | stock or broth (not bouillon)
stoned | pitted

tart tin | tart pan
tea towel | dish towel
tomato purée | tomato paste

vanilla pod | vanilla bean

Acknowledgements

I put all the people who mean the most to me on the back page. Quite frankly, these people will always have my back.

BIG TENKS to Kamil, the real OG, the BBQ specialist, the man, the myth, the legend. Love you Kamil. Arif and Esin: Arif probably doesn't know I spent a lot of time trying to be like him but shhh, don't tell him. You guys are alright, Esin will do anything for us, but she will never be blood. Alev and Oli, the power couple. The older I get, the more I get on with Alev. She also once made a cake that tasted like an English breakfast that we still rinse her for. Oli, I couldn't have asked for a better brother-in-law, thank you for introducing us to medium-rare and salt beef bagels all those years ago. Also, thanks for Trav, not too keen on the other one. Joking, Roxy, I love you too. Grandma, for always going that extra mile to make us happy. Uncle Vic, for all the facts on things you never knew you needed to know.

A special thank you to my nene, for showing me how important good food is. My dede, for probably naming one of his goats after me.

Hasan Amca and Meyrem Hala, Mustafa Eniste and Sergul Hala ❤ Kemal Amca and Fatma Yenge, Gulseren Hala and Yalcin Eniste, Nogay Amca, Muhharrem Amca and Julie Yenge, Meyrem Hala and Bekir Eniste and Esen Hala and Latif Eniste, for looking after us on holidays, for treating us like their own kids. For providing love, laughter and great food. To all the cousins, there's bare of us!

Yo the mandem, the guinea pigs, the life jackets, the guys I owe bare money to.

Tayfun – last name Ramsey – the manager. Ty rings me three times a week to see that I'm on track and if I've got money coming in. The guy who always checks if I've got drinks in my fridge. Thank you for running me around to buy ingredients.

Hus – that's my right hand, the bank, the go-to, the plug. Hus has had my back for years and will remain until the day I die. Five years ago, people would stop me and be like, 'You're Hus' boy, innit?' How the tables have turned mate. We should all be more like Hus, not giving an absolute fuck, doing what we want and living life.

Nawaz – from teaching me to tie a tie on the first day of school, to always daring me to do shit and getting me in trouble in D&T. Nawaz is actually my most level-headed friend and the one I will always go to for advice on real-life situations. My marketing man, the LA jet-setting bad boy. Love you, bro.

Robert – Robert is my oldest friend, me and Rob are batty and bench. All the buzzing convos about the future. The maddest thing is that everything I ever told Rob is slowly happening. Maybe Robert's secretly a wizard or something. Thanks for always backing a BBQ and always answering your phone for a chat my guy x

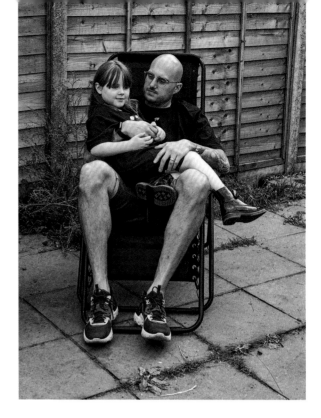

Tre – I've never met a prettier man in my life, nor have I ever met a man who lacked common sense who's got 12 GCSEs – until the day I die, I will never understand it. Thank you for opening up your house to me as a kid bro. Tre's the reason why I'm secretly a Yardie.

Nick – the back-garden Wembley, left-footed magician, the man who owns more basketball jerseys than JD, the 80s movie fiend. Large up Nick, thank you for letting me DJ back in the purple Corsa days.

Listen, I'm lucky to have these knobs in my life. These guys aren't just friends, they're family members, they're my peoples, the uncles to my unborns. I love and appreciate you all. When I'm eating, we're all eating, I promise.

I can't not talk about the chefs I've worked with, the chefs that showed me everything, the people I've spent more time with than my family. I owe you lot.

Jamie Oliver for building Fifteen, for taking a risk to help out people like me, for being in my life still up until the day. Big Love.
My Brazilian dad, Almir Santos.
Every Fifteen graduate.
The foundation team, large up the ladies.
Stevie Parle, for just letting me do and say what I like.
Alex Jackson, the captain of all things France.
Barnaby Benbow, whose obsession with butter was borderline romantic.
Elliot Thomas, the kiwi magician.
Massy, for just listening to me chat shit all the time.
Richard Blackwell, for showing me how to become a sous chef and showing me the ropes.
Cornish Ryan, for having my back always.
Elliot Cunningham, the smoke wizard and all-round great guy.
And anyone else I ever worked with. Big up you lot. Even the ones that are complete knobs.

The boys at Swaledale for providing the meat.
The team at Steve Hatts who easily have the best

seafood in London. Natoora for delivering to me, even though I'm miles away. Miles at Drumbecue, for the beautiful drum. Lord logs for the charcoal and chats about life.

Molly Blunt for the sickest collages. Big up you for buying this book. All of you lot that watch Sunday Sessions, I love you.

A special thank you to the team at Pit magazine who gave me the opportunity to write the way I wanted. The two most important women in my life – Grace O'Leary and Frankie Lyell.

Big up George for backing Sunday Sessions in the arctic weather, even though we don't make money out of it yet.

Everyone at Pavilion – Cara Armstrong for making this shit happen, Laura Russell for styling and washing up almost the entire day. Max and Liz who shot the book; everything is great and you're great fun to be around.

Pavilion
An imprint of HarperCollinsPublishers Ltd
1 London Bridge Street
London SE1 9GF

www.harpercollins.co.uk

HarperCollinsPublishers
1st Floor, Watermarque Building
Ringsend Road Dublin 4
Ireland

10 9 8 7 6 5 4 3 2 1

First published in Great Britain by
Pavilion, an imprint of HarperCollinsPublishers Ltd 2022

Copyright © Hasan Semay 2022

Hasan Semay asserts the moral right to be identified as
the author of this work. A catalogue record for this
book is available from the British Library.

ISBN 978-1-911682-35-6

MIX
Paper from
responsible sources
FSC
www.fsc.org
FSC™ C007454

This book is produced from independently certified
FSC™ paper
to ensure responsible forest management.

For more information visit:
www.harpercollins.co.uk/green

Reproduction by Rival Colour Ltd, UK
Printed and bound in Latvia

Commissioning Editor: Cara Armstrong
Copy Editor: Vicky Orchard
Proofreader: Vicki Murrell
Indexer: Isobel McLEan
Photographer: Haraala Hamilton
Food Styling: Hasan Semay
Prop Stylist: Charlie Phillips
Design Manager: Laura Russell
Artworks: Molly Blunt

Please take care when working with fire and ensure that
you, others, and any property are adequately protected
from flames and smoke. Do not work with fire for the
first time without supervision from an appropriately
experienced person. When using kitchen appliances
please always follow the manufacturer's instructions.

**Here's a little playlist of the tunes I had running in the
background whilst writing this book, listen in for the
full, immersive HOME experience. Has x**